O.K.
YOU MUGS

O.K. YOU MUGS

Writers on Movie Actors

EDITED BY

Luc Sante and
Melissa Holbrook Pierson

Granta Books
London

Granta Publications, 2/3 Hanover Yard, London N1 8BE

First published in Great Britain by Granta Books 2000

Preface copyright © 1999 by Luc Sante and Melissa Holbrook Pierson

The authors have asserted their moral rights under the Copyright, Designs
and Patents Act, 1988, to be identified as the authors of this work.

A CIP catalogue record for this book
is available from the British Library.

1 3 5 7 9 10 8 6 4 2

ISBN 1 86207 362 7

Printed and bound in Great Britain by Mackays of Chatham plc

Page 269 constitutes a continuation of the copyright page.

CONTENTS

Contents

Contents

PREFACE

Actors are our spectral friends. They are figures who loom in our lives as large as or maybe even larger than our actual acquaintances, but with an important difference: they don't know who we are.

But how intimately we know them! Sitting front-row-not-quite-center you seem to inhabit the left nostril of the male lead; you may raise an arm to wave away the smoke rings now obscuring the starlet's lips. When the lights go up—go ahead, admit it—you walk up the aisle with your hips tilted just so (like hers), your eyebrow cocked in that same know-it-all look. Some of it is a simple taking up of arms against the light, against The End. But some of it is the desire to have a life that big, that well described, that fully lived, that well understood. And so we bring them home with us, to populate our dreams, bidden or not. We take them along with us to work and dinner and on walks and car rides, and discuss them with others. We wonder if they can possibly be as brilliant and seductive, or as feeble and shallow, as they appear on the screen. We talk about them as if they were their roles, half the time, as if they were doing their own casting and writing their own scripts. We

conceive crushes on this one and that one, without being terribly sure whether the desire applies to the human being, the fictional character, or an amalgamation of the two.

To pry them apart, indeed, would mean to rip away the very heart of the movies, to reduce the transforming power of film to sprocket holes and running time. No. Two hours in the dark can instead be nothing less than a life or a lesson or a trip. From the seats in the audience we project our desire to be wildly misled—and our faith that we are about to be—onto the director's clay. But it is the actor who comes along to blow breath into the homunculus, to make it throb and jump, and of course to reflect our desire back at us. That latter quality is why the art of the movie actor is so different in essence from that of his counterpart on the stage. The movie actor is not just up there on a screen; he is himself a screen. A movie actor may lack all the classic dramatic skills—diction, rhythm, grace—and still be powerfully effective. What is required is the ability to be a receptacle for all the sundry emotional baggage thrown up from the seats and then to send it back, subtly unpacked.

The movies erase distance. Our stand-ins, up there on the screen that is now inseparable from our own eyes, are us, only better, or worse, or different. Always different. The chance to be someone else for a brief spell makes us happier even than, say, finding an unexpected check in the mail. We owe effusive thanks to actors both quick and dead for this amazing gift. But our gratitude is not actually won by some vague "someone else"—it is offered to Thelma, to Warren, to Jean. This is both a sadness and a cause for joy, because their very specificity, that which causes us to be able to merge lives there in the dark, is what is gone when they are. *No one* looks like her, or talks like him, no one. After you've walked a mile in their shoes, you really know what you're losing. The great movie actors are as singular as they are permeable. Some, though, are more singular than others. There are stars and then there are stars. From the very beginning of motion pictures, when popular favorites did not even have names (Florence Lawrence, for example, was for years known only as "The Biograph Girl"), there have been boy and girl ideals who were primarily pretty. They were so permeable they essentially boiled down to a dimple or a set of teeth. The byways of film history are littered with the husks of forgotten sweetie pies who kept the cash registers ringing in their time but evaporated like any fad.

In contrast, there have also always been actors who are so irreducibly themselves they can be inserted anywhere. A few of these are stars, but most fall under that near-euphemistic heading of "character actors." They are selected for their roles because they are not gorgeous enough for the leads, or because their noses have been broken one too many times, or because teenage acne and a Bronx upbringing have left unexpungeable marks. In short, they are real. The designations often blur, of course. It was said of Cary Grant that although he was a star by virtue of his looks, he was skilled enough to have been a character actor. And on just which side of the fence does Jean Arthur fall, anyway? Besides, there are second leads, professional villains, period specialists, reaction-shot specialists, double-take artists, actors who get hauled in whenever the script calls for a judge or a bookie or a society matron, actors who are foxes (they do too many things well to leave a specific impression), and actors who are hedgehogs (they can do only one thing, but they've cornered the market on it).

And this is what keeps us coming back, hoping they will keep coming back. As they reappear in one film and then another, it is as if they are returning in our very dreams: these characters take on character. You see an actor in enough pictures, you start to compile a biography, you get a sense of a complete and rounded personality at work, one that goes beyond character. Of course, you are indeed seeing a distinct personality on the job over a period of years, and as the movies pile up into a simulacrum of life, so do the events taking place in the downtime between camera appearances. This phenomenon causes confusion often enough, and not just in dewy-eyed teenyboppers. Actors lead two lives, one on and one off, and the personalities they display in each are not likely to be the same or even necessarily similar. But this imaginary life, and the coherence it can manage despite changes of location and costume and even century, is an important aspect of the movie actor's work, often more significant than any particular role. There are major-performance actors who never succeeded in constructing a persona (think Paul Muni), others who created an indelible persona without ever playing a specific part that left much of an impression (somebody like Robert Keith, who appeared in dozens of movies, usually as the father, so that the moment we see him, we think: "the father"). Actors who develop personae can become familiars, commonplaces, semiotic markers, figures out of Greek mythology. They may not always be stars, but they are bigger than life, because they so completely embrace it in all its trademark oddities and imperfections.

Film, as the newest art, has amassed an unusually ripe pile of theoretical approaches, offered in apology for its short and unabashedly popular life. As a kind of religion, it naturally beckons to theologians aching to account for its force and to harness it by means of a structure. These theories have given off the important scent of formalism, structuralism, Marxism, semiotics—primarily European-derived perfumes designed to elevate the senses into the clouds. All of these theories are perfectly correct. Sergei Eisenstein was right just as André Bazin was right just as Christian Metz was right, and their successors and epigones are also right. Cinema is vast and can effortlessly absorb any number of conflicting ideas. But in the end, the only reason to watch the movies (unless they are mere exercises in formalism or structuralism or . . .) is that in the dark it always comes down to just you and that mug up there on the screen. And so the approach that bridges the span from the cave-dwelling days before theory to the post-theory fatigue of the present is finally the personal one.

The personal approach is not in conflict with nor a rebuke to theory. It registers affinities, judges specific works or performances according to the rules they themselves purport to follow, focuses at all times on the particular, with no thought of a northwest passage or a philosophers' stone. Since it abjures received ideas it tends to see film as a plastic medium and so avoids the literary cast that disfigures so much nontheoretical writing on film—the kind that treats movies as if they were

illustrated books. There is a rich American tradition of lucid
writing on the movies, beginning in the 1930s with Otis Fer-
guson, continuing in the following decade with James Agee
and Manny Farber, three writers whose ability to concentrate
upon, convey, and argue with what they actually saw before
them on the screen makes you wonder what most of their con-
temporaries were going on about.

Indeed, that dumbfounding clarity is located in the certainty of an I who believes in the eye as the portal to mysteries
that hitherto looked plain, as well as plain things that suddenly
reveal themselves to be mysterious. Or, in other words, it is
voiced only by someone who is confident of his voice. The
essays collected here, each with its own peculiar timbre, speak
as individuals with something to say about being individuals.
Not unsurprisingly, they take as their subjects those movie
actors who became known for being the kind of individual you
could call in to provide the generic color only a complete individual could provide; largely character actors, they filled in
background even as they stood out and called, perhaps, your
name.

One doesn't usually think of acting as a solitary pursuit, but
it is. With others all around, the great ones—and that, by the
way, includes the ones you may never have heard of—have,
like writers, built an entire cosmos within themselves, and
their art consists in part of projecting it outward. You might
think it a strange thing to say that actors don't often get their
due in print, considering the thousands of acres of trees felled
each year to convey piffle about hairstyles and lifestyles and
styles in inebriation. The fact remains that too little gets writ-

ten about what actors actually do on the screen, and of that little, most of it consists of observations of the same Chaplins and Marilyns as ever. This book is instead dedicated to the proper investigation of the screen's ordinary Joes, those who therefore render themselves extraordinary. A few exceptions represent those universally deemed extraordinary (e.g., Liz Taylor) but who, with a talent for reversal, manage to render themselves ordinary by their insistent wanderings through the realm of the personal. The point always, however, is to listen for the whisper that emanates from the theater's speakers but seems intended for one's ears alone. Thus this book collects stories that are nothing so much as romances: awash in the occult peculiarities of individual attraction. Who can explain such chemistry? Trust a writer to try.

This century belongs to the cinema; it is the lingua franca of our age. Those who speak its varied accents are our emotional government. Actors aren't elected, but they wind up representing us whether we like it or not. We're shackled to the screen even if we don't go to the movies much, seeing everything in our lives projected up there, seeing the movie of this minute as it happens, feeling simultaneously inflated and deflated by the impression. So actors aren't just artists we admire, or fantasy love objects, or chessmen in some strange game—they're us, a bigger us. They spook us, stalk us, fulfill us or fail to. Whatever it is, it's an intimate relationship. Let's break it down.

Melissa Holbrook Pierson and Luc Sante
Brooklyn, November 1998

O.K.
YOU MUGS

TIMOTHY CAREY

Chris Tsakis

My head is too fucking large. My eyes . . . Jesus. The lids droop. I look sleepy all the time. My nose is okay, a little big but not all that out of proportion. I can't breathe with it too well so my mouth hangs open most of the time. Gives me the look of an idiot or a criminal. Or an idiot criminal.

When I smile my thin lips pull taut against my gums and I end up grimacing. I always end up grimacing. Like a creep.

I don't like looking at myself too much but this beard and mustache is a new thing for me. I can't decide if I like it or not. I think I'll shave it as soon as this fucking picture is wrapped. If it's *ever* wrapped.

I like my hair alright. It's thick and seems to be staying where it belongs. I ain't going bald, anyway. I got my grandfather's hair and it pisses my old man off something fierce. Fuck him, too.

Even with the full head of hair this is not what you'd call an attractive face. Mean. Bony. Like a horse's. Not a leading man's face. I'll never be a leading man. Not the romantic hero, the best friend, the standup guy. If they want a scumbag, they call me. I can give them the best fucking scumbag you ever saw.

Need a bouncer to chase James Dean away from the bordello where his mother works? Call me. Need a nasty biker? Call me. Need a guy to shoot a horse? Need a coward? Call me.

That's enough of this staring at myself shit. Fuck, I can't stand vain men. Guys who study themselves in the mirror, guys who worry about every damn wrinkle. Guys in this business.

Kirk is almost like that. He's almost *too* concerned with his appearance. The tyranny of the face is known only to the leading man. And Kirk is a leading man if ever there was one. He's not as bad as some I've known. Brando—now *there* was a prima donna—couldn't walk past a mirror without admiring himself. Worse than Dean. Half a fag, if you ask me. Marvin wanted to actually kick the shit out of him, not just pretend for the camera. He comes to me one day with a bottle of bourbon, still in his Chino getup, and says, "Howsabout when the cameras start rolling I actually clean Marlon's fucking clock?" I said, "Go ahead, Lee—they'll throw you off the picture and I'll angle for your part." That shut him up pretty fast.

Christ, I have to call Marvin. We're supposed to get together and play some poker one of these nights. But he's a hell of a lot busier than I am these days. Even if he's almost as ugly as me. We were bitching to each other about the parts we get because of our faces. I was much more pissed off about it than he was. "I ain't ugly . . ." he said, in that booming voice, ". . . I got character." We laughed. I laughed harder. I've adopted that line for myself. "I ain't ugly . . ."

Fucking yes I am.

And Hollywood knows it. A bunch of one-dimensional shits. Every movie is a silent movie, a fucking cartoon. Guy on the screen supposed to be capable, good-hearted, and virtuous? Get some tall pretty boy with a strong chin. Guy supposed to be a thief, a louse, a filthy piece of shit? Call Carey!

They cast me when they want the ugliness to show through, the ugliness they think I have in my heart. They don't know what's in my heart. They don't give a shit. "Get that ugly fuck Carey!" they probably shout. "We got a stupid scumbag we want him to play."

In my experience—stupid scumbag that I am—most beautiful people have the ugliest souls. They never have to do anything but stand around being admired, catered to, ass-kissed. As long as their looks hold they'll always have work, always have someone telling 'em just how great they are.

But I'm not beautiful. I'm a "character" actor. Which is a polite term for an ugly guy or gal who's gonna die or kill someone or otherwise provide some "color."

Like on this film. I'm a prisoner. A coward. A pawn. I'm going up in front of a firing squad for being yellow. But this movie's not about me, even though I get shot through the fucking heart. It's about Kirk, about Colonel Dax and his moral goddamn dilemma. You can tell he's good—just look at his face! Meanwhile, me and two other guys are being put to death 'cause we're ugly bastards. Because we *look* like cowards, mostly.

Fucking hot in here. Even sitting in front of the fan it's hot. Up at six this morning, on the set at seven and now it's ten and

I still haven't done a fucking thing. Just sitting around smoking cigarettes. Hurry up and wait, hurry up and wait.

I hate this costume they got me in—it itches like hell. Where's my cigarettes? There's no pockets in this goddamn thing. I wish they'd hurry up and get this damn shot set up. I can't stand the goddamn waiting while Kubrick makes everything just so. The man is a motherfucking perfectionist. I've been in plenty of fucking movies and no one works like this guy. He takes hours just to set lights, for Christ's sake. What's the big deal? Just some ugly guys getting shot.

Christ, I have to fart. Fart proudly, Benjamin Franklin said. Me too. A fart never killed anyone, unless you keep it in. Just let it go. Even so, I don't want to fart in front of Kubrick. He doesn't seem like a guy who appreciates a good fart. I bet he goes into his trailer when he has to break wind. So proper. Weird fucking guy.

He hasn't said much to me. Just told me that this guy I'm playing is a little slow, maybe a coward, maybe not. When we were shooting the *The Killing* he sat down with me and told me the guy I was going to play was—guess what?—a coward. "He'll do anything to get by," he said. Well, not anything. The guy wouldn't work a legitimate job. He'd steal, he'd murder . . . cut whatever corners he has to. Why? Just look at his face. Ugly fuck.

I was so ugly I had to call that poor parking lot attendant a nigger when all the kid wanted to do is be friends. I didn't want to call him a nigger, but I had to get rid of the kid before that horse came into the open. I was supposed to shoot the horse from my car—shit, you've seen the picture—as a diversion from the robbery and the kid won't leave me alone so I snap at him and call him "nigger." I got such shit for that part. I got a guy who wanted to punch my lights out 'cause he confused me with the guy in the movie. And the guy in the movie got *shot*. Shot dead.

What am I doing in this business? Feeding the fucking stereotype, I suppose.

I stuck my ugly, stereotypical face in front of Stanley's just this morning. I said, "Stanley, they got me dying quietly in this script. I want to make some noise, for Christ's sake. I don't want to die quietly." He said he'd think about it. What the hell is there to think about? Put me in front of a firing squad on a trumped-up charge and I'd have plenty to say about it, ugly face or no ugly face.

Christ, I'm bored. I'm bored to tears. And my head is pounding. I'm trying to imagine what it would be like to be shot to death and all I can muster is this damn headache. My neck is completely stiff, too. I wish we could get this thing over with already. I want to be shot now.

Just got the call to the set. This is it. Final makeup adjustment, final costume adjustment, Stanley comes over, tells me to react however I'd like when it's time for the close-up. How would I react if there were a bunch of guys with guns pointed at me, ready to fire? I wouldn't stand there with my big ugly mouth shut. I would plead for my life. I would blubber. I would break down.

I like life too much to have it taken away like this. I'll go kicking and screaming. They'll see the fear in my eyes, the terror on my face, they'll know they're doing the wrong thing. I'll make them know. It'll be all over my face—my ugly face.

Oh yeah. I ain't ugly—I got character.

Now to die.

May 11, 1994—Timothy Carey, 65, a heavy-eyed character actor who often played villains and whose films ranged from Paths of Glory *and* One-Eyed Jacks *to 1960s beach movies, died today at a hospital in Los Angeles after a stroke.*

MITCHUM GETS OUT OF JAIL

Dave Hickey

Robert Mitchum died this summer at the age of seventy-nine. Twenty-four hours later, Jimmy Stewart died, as well, and I choose to see the Hand of Providence at work in this, since the prospect of Jimmy Stewart in a world without Robert Mitchum is not one I like to contemplate. In fact, just imagining the world without Mitchum is hard enough, since my earliest memories of the popular landscape are of a world with *only* Mitchum in it. This was in the late nineteen forties and early fifties, when I was a kid, and Mitchum *was* the counter-culture—a one-man Zeitgeist. In the bland, herbivorous pasture of popular entertainment, he was the single, successful, visible icon of America's dark inheritance. Others had tried to bring that darkness out of the closet, only to be cast back into it. Mitchum brought it out, stuck it in the face of nice America, and got away with it.

Among the likes of Jimmy Stewart, Henry Fonda, and Ronald Reagan, he was like a switchblade on a plate of cupcakes. For my friends and me, however, Mitchum was a familiar spirit—our adopted "rambling uncle"—someone we knew, and for whom we had some sympathy. We had never seen any

creatures like him on the screen before, but we had seen them down at the filling station, so we recognized Mitchum for what he was: jailhouse aristocracy—the best of the worst—a loser with a winner's heart. However often he fell, he would remain a "stand-up" guy, we knew. He would never snitch off a friend, or pardon his failings with some lame excuse, or ever, ever change. That was the glory of jailhouse aristocrats: They could be killed, but they could not be defeated. The pity was, they rarely ever won.

Even in the movies, in the magic mirror of desire, jailhouse honor could only triumph if the hero died. So, for a while there, Mitchum was always dying in the last reel. "That's me," he said of these roles, "dead but undefeated." In life, however, nose to nose with propriety, armed only with his wit and aplomb, Mitchum proved a lot harder to kill. Disasters that would have extinguished other careers just fed the flames for Mitchum. In 1948, just as his career was catching fire, he was nabbed in the first Major Celebrity Drug Bust, for marijuana, at a house up in Laurel Canyon. Standing before the booking sergeant in handcuffs that night, he was asked to state his occupation. "Former actor," Mitchum said without a blink. The reporters wrote that down, and the next morning, people all over the country, prepared to be incensed by Mitchum's drugged-out wickedness, laughed out loud.

He did sixty days, stand-up, at the county farm and emerged larger than life. "What's it like 'inside'?" one reporter asked. "Just like Palm Springs," Mitchum said, "without the riffraff, of course." When the requisite *mea culpa* was demanded of him, he said, "Well, I'm not stupid, and I don't plan to get into any more trouble. But who can say what I might do tomorrow? If I put out some phony reform story and then fall from grace, I'll just look like a liar." That was Mitchum: Know yourself, privilege veracity over virtue, behave with absolute plausibility. Henceforth, nobody expected anything of him, except that he be Mitchum, and Mitchum, of course, remained a mystery behind his sleepy gaze.

So there were always surprises. A few years later, he precipitated the first great *paparazzo momento,* when the Euro-starlet with whom he was posing on the beach at Cannes suddenly dropped her bikini top. Mitchum, with whimsical gallantry, restored her modesty by covering her breasts with his hands. The cameras popped, and there it was: *Major American movie star holding two formidable, naked, foreign, female breasts!* For an amiable herbivore like Jimmy Stewart, this would have been suicide. For Mitchum, it was *no problemo,* because of his jailhouse cool, his psychological unavailability—which, in truth, is a lot like Oscar Wilde's, in that they both do "moments," confrontational situations in which we glimpse, not the secret self, but the embodied attitude. So what we get is the *performance:* the perfect gesture and the shrewd *aperçu,* not so much expressed as delivered—and Mitchum could deliver a line. My favorite, from a movie, is in *His Kind of Woman* (1951).

JANE RUSSELL: I hear you killed Ferraro. How does it feel?

MITCHUM: He didn't tell me.

Then, in 1958, Mitchum transcended the status of "rambling uncle" for me and my pals. He produced and starred in *Thunder Road*, the first authentic "cult-teen-*noir.*" He also wrote and sang the title song. In case you don't remember, *Thunder Road* was a broody little black-and-white about a doomed hot-rodder driving illegal whiskey through the mountains of the mid-South, and as we sat together in the old Majestic and watched it, everything we always knew was out there—the whole dark, sleazy romance—oozed around the edges of the screen. Later that night, around a table at the Toddle House, we just gave up and admitted that nobody was cooler than Mitchum. Not even *Elvis* was cooler than Mitchum, and thus it was, in recognition of this fact, that I made the best decision I have ever made in my life: I decided that if I only dated women who thought Robert Mitchum was cool, I would be okay—and, amazingly enough, as long I did, I was, and still am.

This may sound like a joke, but I'm being perfectly serious. This is what culture does: It correlates us in relation to one another. So, again and again, applying the Mitchum test, I found myself in sexy, dangerous, kaleidoscopic relationships that, somehow, at their heart, were grounded in calm equanimity. When, on the other hand, hormones and ambition drove me to ignore the Mitchum test, I immediately found myself adrift, lost and confused in alien latitudes of the gene pool. So the Mitchum test worked, like a charm, and I still don't know why. Nor do I know what it says about Mitchum or myself or the women who found us both presentable. I only know that I owe Mitchum big time, and, for some reason, I eluded every chance I had to meet him and maybe compliment him in person on the vivacity of his female fans.

I have been thinking about this a lot since his death, because I could have done it, you know, and nearly did a number of times. I have friends who wrote for him and about him, friends who worked on films with him and sold paintings to him, but for some reason, whenever the opportunity arose, I shied away. Upon reflection, I think it was because the privacy of Mitchum's private life was a part of the public magic for me—the *terra incognita* whose present absence lent his persona its subversive weight. Because whenever Mitchum is on camera or on tape, in character or in person, in word or in deed, he always seems to be declaring the primacy of things we do not know about him.

So, I didn't want to see the private Mitchum plain because I loved the shadowy, refracted glimpses one caught in his public manner. That is the "Mitchum effect"—that jailhouse thing— the commanding physical presence, the cool demeanor, the suppressed inference of a spirit and a sensibility whose unavailability is the key to its appeal. You *know* there is something back there, driving the engine, paying careful attention from a remote vantage point, but you don't know what it is. So, whatever Mitchum does on the screen, in person or as a character, seems at once surprising and plausible—full of potential power and menace, whimsy and *élan*.

Peter O'Toole can do this, too, and he describes it in similar terms: There are actors, O'Toole says, who construct a character out of details, who make you believe their characters by constructing a plausible narrative for them, and then there are actors who *are* plausible, in their bodies, who can invest anything they choose to do with plausibility, who *make* you believe it. O'Toole and Mitchum are actors of the latter sort, and, in truth, what they do is not really *acting* at all; it is more like performing with a vengeance, physically convincing us that the actions we see arise from a coherent source to which we have no access, and cannot understand.

To see the difference, watch Robert De Niro and Mitchum playing the same character, the rapacious Max Cady in the two versions of *Cape Fear.* De Niro's performance is very good and perfectly explicable. You understand the character because it is artfully constructed and powerfully enacted, but you *believe* Mitchum. He's *really* scary, because we don't understand, we only sense that the character's behavior arises from some plausible, fucked-up rat's nest of damaged intention lurking somewhere back in the shadows. So we are always surprised and we believe it when we are, and we are afraid of being surprised again. For De Niro, the text is a vehicle; for Mitchum, the text is a jail, and by treating it as a jail, Mitchum effortlessly subverts the niceties of popular narrative.

Mitchum is always playing a presence, a moral creature, incarcerated by the text, and when it works, he burns a hole in the screen, invests the vacant platitudes of professional screenwriting with something dark and strange, simply because he is not playing by the rules: He is *obeying* the rules, of course, as any convict must. He is hitting his marks, making the moves and saying the words, but he is not *acting* by the rules, not deriving the subtext from the text. Like Coltrane playing a standard, he is investing the text with his own sub-versive vision, his own pace and sense of dark contingency. So what we see in a Mitchum performance is less a character por-trayed than a propositional alternative: What if someone with Mitchum's sensibility grew up to be a sea captain? a private eye? a schoolteacher? Mitchum puts himself, literally and physically, into the part, which would be boring if we knew who Mitchum was, but we don't. He remains a stranger in a world where everyone's a stranger.

A few years ago, I was sitting in a friend's loft in Soho watching Robert Mitchum on a local talk show, and as always, Mitchum was being wonderfully watchable. He was promoting a movie, but the interviewer was one of those well-dressed Broadway queens who like to schmooze on subjects like "the actor's craft," and Mitchum (who could talk about anything) was obliging. At one point, the interviewer asked him about the dif-ference between movie-acting and stage-acting. Mitchum thought for a minute and said the difference was that the audi-ence watching a movie believes what they're seeing is real. "Not the story," he said, waving his hand, "but the setting and the props, the *mise en scène*. Movies ask us to believe that stuff is real, and we do, because usually it is.

"If I'm on location, shooting a scene where I'm leaning against a tree, the tree is real; the sky behind it is the real sky; the ground I'm standing on is real dirt. The clothes I'm wear-ing are what the character would wear in that situation, and they're real, too. If I'm carrying a gun, which I often do, it's a real gun. Everything is real, in other words, except *me*, my character. That's fake. It's a made-up person. So you have to use the audience's belief in the setting and the props to make the character real. I'll give you an example: Most actors handle guns on screen like they're cap-pistols or they blow bubbles. They are real guns, of course, but the actors make them fake. They forget that it's a real gun because they're in a movie.

"Now, a real gun is a very serious instrument. It has serious implications and terrible consequences, so you have to handle a gun like that, as if it were serious—as you would handle a very serious thing. If you do this, your character gets real in a hurry—it steals the reality of the gun, which the audience already believes. On stage, it's just the reverse. The setting and props are fake. Or, even if they're real, they look fake. So, it's a completely different thing. Also, the stage is *still*. When you're acting in a film, you know that when people finally see what you're doing, everything will be moving. There will be this hurricane of pictures swirling around you.

"The projector will be rolling, the camera will be panning, the angle of the shots will be changing, and the distance of the shots will be changing, and all these things have their own tempo, so *you* have to have a tempo, too. If you sit or stand or talk the way you do at home, you look silly on the screen, incoherent. On screen, you have to be purposive. You have to be moving or not moving. One or the other. So a lot of times, in a complicated scene, the best thing to do is stand *absolutely* still, not moving a muscle. This would look *very* strange if you did it at the grocery store, but it looks okay on screen because the camera and the shots are moving around you.

"Then, when you do move, even to pick up a teacup, you

have to move *at a speed*. Everything you do has to have pace, and if you're the lead in a picture, you want to have the pace, to *set* the pace, so all the other tempos accommodate themselves to yours. In a furious action scene, for instance, if you move a little more slowly and a little more deliberately, you control the tempo. Everyone else looks out of control. Or, let's say your character is standing on a bluff looking at a sunset. The sunset is big and still, so if you move—just glance around or resettle yourself on your feet—the sunset wins. You look weak. If you *don't* move, you control the sunset. If that's what you want to do.

"So that's movie acting. You steal the reality of the props and control the pace of the pictures. Oh, also, you have to say these lines, but that's purely secondary. You try not to stutter or drool or blink too much. Otherwise, it's pace and props. If you have the tempo and people believe you in the setting, they'll believe whatever you say, however you say it, if they hear it. So I always try to speak slowly and very clearly, because I'm a baritone and have a lot of melisma in my voice. And that's it. One take. It's not easy, but it's not hard, either. What's hard is believing what you're doing will work when it's finally on the screen. It's more like riding a horse than what they teach at the Dramatic Academy."

And that's it: Mitchum's theory of acting. I have elaborated on his exposition here, to compensate for the absence of Mitchum's delivery, but this is the sense of what he said. I wrote it down in my notebook that night and considered it a very nice gift. It was like finally understanding, with a little help from the artist, why a painting has been breaking your heart all these years—and understanding, as well, that there is something to understand, that it isn't just charisma. Then, a couple of nights later, in that same loft, I saw the theory in practice. I was watching *The Yakuza*, a 1975 film in which Mitchum plays an American involved with the Japanese underworld.

Late in the movie, there is a scene in which Mitchum and his Japanese costar, Takakura Ken, are approaching the gangster's headquarters at night, moving through a dark garden. Ken is holding a sword at his waist. Mitchum is carrying a shotgun. They are both slightly crouched and moving at a pace through the darkness. Then, as they descend a shallow embankment, Mitchum's pace breaks; he seems to overbalance for an instant, and with a little jerk of his hand, he shifts his grip on the shotgun, tests the balance of its weight, and moves on with authority. And in that split second, as Mitchum would put it, the scene gets real in a hurry. We sense the weight of the gun, its reality and seriousness, the anxiety of moving in the dark toward danger, the purposefulness of the characters. Everything in the action sequence that follows draws its *frisson* from the authority of Mitchum adjusting the weight of the gun, that little hitch in the flow of movement. So I have been thinking about it, testing it in my mind, and on the whole, Mitchum seems to have come up with a pretty good theory: Touch the world. Set the pace. Fuck the text. *À bientôt*, Robert.

ENDLESS MELODY STARRING
Jonathan Williams

Mickey Rooney, as Carl Sandburg
Lon Chaney, Jr., as Robert Frost
Edward Everett Horton, as T. S. Eliot
Thomas Mitchell, as Ezra Pound
MacDonald Carey, as William Carlos Williams
Myrna Loy, as Mina Loy
Martha Raye, as Marianne Moore
Adolphe Menjou, as Edward Dahlberg
Keenan Wynn, as Walter Lowenfels
Fred Astaire, as Louis Zukofsky
Robert Mitchum, as Kenneth Patchen
Brian Donlevy, as Kenneth Rexroth
Bert Lahr, as Henry Miller
Cary Grant, as James Laughlin
Gene Autry, as Lawrence Ferlinghetti
Oscar Levant, as Allen Ginsberg
Rod Cameron, as Jack Kerouac
Burl Ives, as Charles Olson
Montgomery Clift, as Robert Creeley
Elvis Presley, as Robert Duncan

Margaret O'Brien, as Denise Levertov
William Bendix, as Irving Layton
   and special guest stars
Peter Lorre, as Oscar Williams
Vincent Price, as Randall Jarrell
Boris Karloff, as Ivor Winters

BARBARA PAYTON: A MEMOIR

Robert Polito

For a few years during the early 1960s my father tended bar at The Coach and Horses on Sunset, in Hollywood. Weekdays he inventoried the sale of stamps, money orders, and Pitney Bowes Machines as supervisor of a Santa Ana post office, close to where he lived in a tidy dingbat studio. But I was about to turn thirteen, and he hoped to send me to a "real college." The post office discouraged second jobs for government employees of his rank, so my father moonlighted only at bars, all transactions cash.

The Coach and Horses lured patrons with the natty coat of arms of a British pub, but inside the landscape registered saloon. This was residential Hollywood. Cocktail lounges unattached to hotels or eateries still tended to be rare in Los Angeles, and survived on local drunks who could swing the tab—well drinks sixty-five cents. Fourteen stools along a runty bar, half as many booths strung in a miniature railroad, the vibes at The Coach and Horses read dark: dusky paneling, blackout drapes, shaded lamps. Haul in a couple of slot machines and you might feel transported to Vegas, even Barstow.

■ ■ ■

The summer of 1962 my father let me join him for his Saturday stints. My parents already were separated, and he took custody of me weekends. In the beginning I was too shy to connect with anyone but him, but I loved the overheard chatter, wisecracks, complaints, the provocative fragments of confessions. The silent drinkers, draining the day over the *Citizen-News*, I also admired, because they were harder to figure out. I read novels and music magazines sitting at a desk in the ruins of an office that the staff tagged the "Black Hole of Calcutta," up a shaky flight of stairs at the back; or sometimes I moved to the last booth, where we covertly replaced the mood lighting with a forty-watt bulb—still too dim to menace the perpetual twilight. We made a day of it, before heading off to supper and a movie. The whole experience was a lot like going to a loud library.

We were about three or four weeks into our routine when a day-manager, probably Rodney, an occasional DJ at Hollywood High dances, started to lecture my father. He felt sorry for me, he said, rotting away doing nothing on another beautiful L.A. afternoon. His concern could also have betrayed the sodden departure the previous night of his latest barback—a fiftyish ex-race car driver fleeing overdue alimony. (The Coach and Horses rotated help nearly every payday.)

Rodney suggested I could better occupy myself. For exactly a dollar less than minimum wage, he put me to work retrieving bottles and splits, sweeping cigarettes off the black-and-red carpeting, soaking glasses. My father and I opened the bar Saturdays at noon. Quickly I graduated also to Friday evenings.

I was too thrilled to tell my mother about my secret employment, but lied cautiously.

Ralph and Leo from Holloway House stopped at The Coach and Horses evenings after work, and Leo usually returned Saturday. Back then, Holloway House—situated up on Holloway Drive—published bottom-feeder Hollywood autobiographies along the lines of *Jayne Mansfield's Wild, Wild World.* Earnestly sensational scientific exposés, such as *Psychodynamics of Unconventional Sex Behavior* by Paul J. Gillette, Ph.D., and unexpurgated classics—*Satyricon: Memoirs of a Lusty Roman*—rounded off the list.

Leo was an old columnist for the *Hollywood Reporter,* a squat mischievous man. He would discover me with a book at the bar during the ordinarily vacant afternoons, and he started to joke with me about school. Leo could talk to anyone.

One day he arrived lugging a fat brick of loose pages— "What's your spelling like?" he quizzed me. His company needed a person to fix galleys. Leo said he was sick of doing everything himself. For exactly a dollar more than minimum wage I signed on as the exclusive proofreader at Holloway House.

This was perfect, since I would now be paid double for reading at The Coach and Horses. The first titles I remember were *Hollywood Screwballs* and *The Many Loves of Casanova.*

The Coach and Horses swirled with legends of famous lushes who boozed there—Hitchcock, Jason Robards, Richard Harris, William Holden. But the only star—if star's the right name for her—we ever saw was Barbara Payton.

Someone, no doubt Leo, told me about "the scandal." Back in the early 1950s Payton was coming off a leading role in *Kiss Tomorrow Goodbye,* when she met B-movie actor Tom Neal at a party. Within days she ended a relationship with Franchot Tone, proclaiming her engagement to Neal. But believing marriage to the more prominent and accomplished Tone might advance her Hollywood stature, Payton ditched Neal—only to return again. "He had a chemical buzz for me that sent red peppers down my thighs," she subsequently explained to *Confidential.* But the night before Payton was to marry Neal, she contrived a date with Tone. Neal waited up for them. The former boxer smashed Tone's nose, and sent him to the hospital with a concussion and fractured cheekbones. Tone secretly underwent plastic surgery.

Payton wed Tone upon his recovery. She divorced him fifty-three days later. Neal and Payton toured in a backwater road production of *The Postman Always Rings Twice,* but both careers derailed.

Connecting *that* Barbara Payton to the woman in The Coach and Horses demanded impossible time travel. Our Barbara Payton oozed alcohol even before she ordered a drink. Her eyebrows didn't match her brassy hair; her face displayed a perpetual sunburn, a map of veins by her nose. Her feet swelled, and she carried an old man's potbelly that sloshed faintly when she moved. Her gowns and dresses looked more like antique costumes than clothes, creased and spotted. She must have weighed two hundred pounds.

She didn't resemble anyone two actors would fight over.

Barbara Payton was then thirty-four years old—younger than my father. She didn't come across as bitter, or angry, or crazy. She clearly wasn't rich, but she always carried ten or twenty dollars for her drinks.

Beyond the rosé, Barbara emanated a chronic self-abdication that outmaneuvered most humiliations. If a new customer of The Coach and Horses wondered whether there might be any regrets, she'd pause, taste her wine, and answer as though she had never considered the question. "You know if I had to do it all over again, I'd do the same. It's all in heaven in a little black book with neat lines. You are what you are and there's no out. You do what you have to do."

She was the first person I met who spoke like she lived in a movie. She conversed through hard-boiled maxims.

"I got news for you baby—nobody's civilized. You peel off a little skin and you got raw flesh."

"But forever is just a weekend—more or less."

She had a theory different sleeping pills will give you different sorts of dreams. She couldn't recall any brand names—only colors: red for passionate dreams; white for horror dreams. Barbara maintained she told this to Gregory Peck while they were filming *Only the Valiant*. He jotted it down.

She enjoyed washing men's dirty shirts—said she liked it the way someone liked playing golf.

Barbara entered The Coach and Horses every Saturday afternoon at five o'clock, and she left at seven, as methodical as a stopwatch conductor. On Fridays she would land around eleven and remain on her stool until we closed at one. Leo sometimes would escort Barbara home—Friday, anyway, but never Saturday, when she always insisted on leaving alone. Her apartment, it turned out, was right on Holloway Drive.

Ralph once joked that Leo could smell a book in a Hollywood toilet. Soon after my proofreading chores started for Holloway House, Leo advanced Barbara Payton $250 for her life story.

He loaned her a tape recorder to reconstruct her memories. A young woman Leo knew named Nancy—I heard later she dated, maybe even married one of the Wilsons, of the Beach Boys—would actually write the text. My job was to transcribe the tapes.

Leo titled Barbara's story after a line she regularly used around the bar: *I Am Not Ashamed.*

I typed on a sleek Remington portable (courtesy of Holloway House) up in the "Black Hole of Calcutta." Barbara's tapes came as a revelation—to me, though hardly, I suspect, to Leo and Ralph. If her Hollywood past loomed a distant mystery, her present amounted to an "other life." Five minutes into the first reel Barbara was describing her practices as a hooker along the Sunset Strip.

On the tapes she compared her book to "a kind of detective story. I—or we—want to find out what happened that started me on the skids, down, down, down, down." Yet Barbara was short on motive or responsibility. Even "the scandal" seemed less a life-transforming watershed than another spongy anecdote.

Barbara herself charted her fall as an inverse pyramid of declining cash. There was stardom, and $10,000 a week. Then, all but inexplicably, no roles—instead $300 "gifts" tactfully deposited inside her purse by producers. Then $100 gifts, left less discreetly on her dresser. She bounced a check at a Hollywood grocery store to purchase liquor. She slept with her landlady's husband for the rent, and on Christmas Eve with an actor friend for $50, then $20 johns, then $10.

Now—her voice woozed from the speaker—"The little money I accumulate comes from old residuals, poetry, and favors to men . . . I love the Negro race and I will accept money only from Negroes . . . White men don't seem to go for me anymore . . . Wine and bare bodies and nightmare sleep and money that was never enough to pay the bills . . . One night I realized I was in bed with a Negro. He was gentle and kind to me . . . He gave me five dollars . . . Five dollars!"

The hooking explained Barbara's meticulous timetable in The Coach and Horses. Friday she drank after she roused a few bucks. Saturday she braced herself against the evening ahead.

The poems, though, appeared to scratch a remnant of pride amid the drift. "I decided it was alright to be a hustler as long as I wrote poetry," Barbara declared on the tapes. "Even in bed with a trick I could think of lines." Her poems zigzagged like her stories—the few poems she showed us. Fragments, essentially: some phrases about Tom Neal, followed by an image from her Texas childhood, ending on a hymn to rosé wine. A writer friend, she mentioned, sold them to a "way-out Beatnik journal" for her.

I asked my father if he knew about Barbara's secret. He laughed. Anything she did was OK, he said, assuming she didn't do it in The Coach and Horses—and provided she stayed away from me.

He did allow Barbara to take me to the movies, twice, each occasion one of her old films. While we were working on the book, *Kiss Tomorrow Goodbye* played at the Oriental, a few doors down Sunset. Another afternoon we rode the bus over to the Encore at Melrose and Van Ness for *Trapped*.

Watching seated alongside Barbara, I was startled by her glamour—slim, blonde, beautiful—and the strangeness of actually knowing someone who made movies.

Seeing those films again, and some others for this history, I'm struck more by her obvious disquiet as an actress. Barbara Payton starred in roughly eleven features between 1949 and 1955, but she flashes anxiously from the margins of her movies. Her presence is fleeting—even when she attained top billing for *Only the Valiant* or *Bride of the Gorilla* her on-screen time amounted to staggered cameos; her command of role is hesitant, uneasy. As Holiday Carleton in *Kiss Tomorrow Goodbye* Payton wobbles from ingenue to she-devil. When facing into the camera she scarcely moves, except her mouth to deliver her lines. Her transitions roll as a succession of production stills, a flip-book of faltering moods.

She does not so much inhabit a character as impersonate a starlet—an act, I suppose, she merely extended to The Coach and Horses, or the Sunset Strip. In her movies Payton is a doll dropped into a scene to insinuate sex. Directors took to filming her from the side, her breasts vaulted in silhouette.

Only Edgar Ulmer understood how to spin her anxiety into an advantage. For *Murder Is My Beat*—Payton's last film—he cast her as Eden Lane, a nightclub singer convicted of murder. On the way to prison Lane is convinced she sees the supposed victim from her train, and escapes. For much of the action the viewer is uncertain whether Lane committed a crime. Payton's tension plays as suspense, her hesitations as possible instability, the intimation that she might indeed be a murderess.

On the tapes Barbara asserted she bankrolled the completion of *Murder Is My Beat* by sleeping with a prosperous stockbroker. "Mr. Shellout" she christened him.

She even put me—or someone like me—into the book. "One night a friend brought over another friend," she suggested, "and the first one left leaving me with this kid. . . . He was so awed by me I went to bed with him and then wouldn't take his money. That's how lousy a hooker I was."

This never happened. But many of Barbara's implausible stories weren't so readily dispelled. She also clutched secrets—her first husband, their son in Texas.

Nancy and I probed, and verified what we could; then we camouflaged the rest against lawsuits. The whole process took us about a month.

I Am Not Ashamed finally appeared in 1963. When Barbara Stanwyck read Payton's autobiography, she reportedly quipped, "Well, she damn well should have been!"

Tom Neal married, and his wife died of cancer. He remarried, and opened a landscaping business in Palm Springs. During a domestic dispute his new wife was shot to death. Like his character Al Roberts at the conclusion of Edgar Ulmer's film *Detour*, Neal maintained the killing was an accident. Barbara attended the trial wearing dark glasses. Neal served six years in the California Institute for Men at Chino before being paroled.

Barbara Payton died of complications from alcoholism in Mexico in 1967. "A blonde movie actress in Mexico," she once said, "is always cause for celebration."

My parents divorced, and my mother never discovered The Coach and Horses. But my father sent me as far east from the bar as possible—to Catholic Boston College. By then he had moved on to the more upscale Firefly Lounge.

Holloway House discovered Iceberg Slim, and everything changed.

DANA ANDREWS,
OR THE MALE MASK

Geoffrey O'Brien

In one of my notebooks from the late 1960s, among disordered notations of dreams and sexual fantasies and barely articulated gothic plot lines, I come upon this passage:

> A man stands in a neon hallway at five in the morning. It is Dana Andrews, in a white trenchcoat, looking at the stairs. He lights a cigarette and thinks the thoughts that make his face that way. A vacant cop whose words are lines of dialogue. An empty trenchcoat—the eyes dead, the body inert—caught in the frame until the reel ends. Vincent Price and Ida Lupino are no longer there to keep him company. He has even lost the photograph of Gene Tierney's eyes.

There is a hiatus, and then the reverie resumes:

> The end of the cigarette. The detective fizzles. Between the office and the alley he becomes a dot. They rip the trenchcoat from his shoulders. The blonde in silk in the

warm room back there flashes an instant against the
empty background and then never comes back. He looks
down and is already ceasing to exist . . .

Vacant, empty, empty, lost, ceasing to exist. Are the words an
attempt to ward off the insistent materiality of the apparition,
to take some of the weight off that implacable cop sprung from
darkness, that hitchhiker adrift among the worlds, unable
either to escape from himself or to stop existing?

How did he get in here anyway, into a psychic space that
elsewhere seems to partake of a late-'60s pipe dream, a bunch
of scattered notes toward an album cover for some late-
blooming Bay Area band just around the time the psychedelic
thing went sour, a spun-sugar paradise of lotus pads and faux
bonsai, Krishna framed among vintage matchbox cover art, a
lamaistic abode drawn for Marvel Comics by a scroll-painter
of the late Ming? Brushing past the wind chimes and coughing
slightly at his first whiff of the incense, this incongruous guy
barges in with his midnight shadow—a case of seriously bad
karma—sleep-deprived, off-kilter, in no mood for discussion.

But that imaginary setting—the sybaritic landscape of an
equally imaginary *satori*—hadn't I seen that somewhere
before? Was it not an adaptation, after all, of Clifton Webb's
luxurious Manhattan apartment in *Laura*, the paradise of chi-
noiserie and discreetly eclectic interior decoration appropriate
to America's most literate and acid-tongued columnist, Waldo
Lydecker?

Indeed, so much began with *Laura*. I shall always remember the day I first heard Clifton Webb intoning, in voice-over, as the camera glides stealthily through an initially bewildering patch of mirrors and curios: "I shall always remember the weekend Laura died." Otto Preminger's 1944 suspense film was capable of marking a spectator almost as profoundly as the title character marked everybody around her. It played often during the 1960s on a double bill with Joseph Mankiewicz's *All About Eve*, thus bringing together, with a kind of inevitability, two great, nearly twin character roles: Clifton Webb as corrosively witty, ultimately loveless columnist Waldo Lydecker, and George Sanders as corrosively witty, ultimately loveless theater critic Addison De Witt. Just as Dana Andrews in *Laura* becomes obsessed—through the medium of a pop tune, endlessly repeated, and an oil portrait, endlessly stared at—with someone irretrievably lost, I was drawn through *Laura*'s tangible elements—voice-over, flashback, title theme, tracking shots, lighting (captured with the brilliant hard-edged focus that distinguished 20th Century Fox movies of that era), sofas, hats, mirrors, clocks, radios, cocktails—into a disturbingly poignant relationship with the vanished 1940s: a time beyond recapture and yet still there to be immersed in, over and over, by means of this very movie.

That opening, with its implication that everything we see is somehow part of the memory of Clifton Webb, becomes even more disorienting with the belated realization that *Laura* does not in fact turn out to be narrated by Webb—indeed could not possibly have been, since he does not outlive its final frame.

His voice guides us just far enough to admit Dana Andrews, as police lieutenant Mark McPherson, into the apartment: "Another of those detectives came to see me . . . I could see him through the half-open door."

Dana Andrews is then at the outset a figure in Clifton Webb's gaze, or more exactly a stooge for Webb's monologue: opaque where Webb is transparent, heavy where Webb is delicate, blunt where Webb is serpentine. The wonder was that this was to be a Hollywood movie filtered through the consciousness of a man who would sit typing in the bathtub and say, to a hard-bitten homicide cop, "Hand me my robe please," or, witheringly, when interrogated about a factual contradiction in one of his columns: "Are the processes of the creative mind now under the jurisdiction of the police?"

As Andrews plays with one of those tiny puzzles whose object is to roll ball bearings into little holes, Webb asks: "Something you confiscated in a raid on a kindergarten?" To which Andrews rejoins, in a first indication of where the real advantage lies: "It takes a lot of control. Would you like to try it?"

Andrews has walked into a den of civilized predators, the realm of bitchy sophistication where Clifton Webb and Judith Anderson and Vincent Price, united by their style of sexual ambivalence and vengeful competitiveness, snarl over the elegant spoils: vases, armoires, classical concerts, tiny Italian restaurants in the Village, and above all the vivacious young girl, Gene Tierney's Laura Hunt—a natural, a diamond in the rough—whose blood might have kept them alive, if only she had not been dead since before the movie began.

In this context Dana Andrews exists so that there might be one person who is not one of these exquisite vampires, a working-class guy who chews gum, speaks his lines with a cigarette jammed in the middle of his mouth, and says things like: "A dame in Washington Heights got a fox fur out of me once." An intruder in the realm of nuance, he submits to mockery only to emerge more triumphantly in the final *règlement de comptes*.

Yet of course he's no different from anyone else, a point underscored visually when Webb, Price, and Andrews walk in single file into Laura's apartment; they look as if they are about to go into a soft-shoe number, "The Three Guys Shuffle" or something of the kind. He has entered this world to investigate her death, and what he learns of in flashback after flashback (each triggered by an upsurge of that diabolically haunting title theme) is her mesmerizing effect on everybody whose path she crossed. It is the narrative itself, its elegant windings and recursions, that takes him over.

He falls in love with the murdered Laura. The emotion must have been gathering force while he sat there listening to all the anecdotes about her singularly penetrating charm, and hearing David Raksin's title theme over and over. Soon he's taken up residence in the apartment, living with her things; listening to her records (or rather record, since she evidently has only that one melody to listen to); virtually becoming the person whose absence it's his job to resolve.

In the dead center of the movie, its witching hour, he sits up all night looking at her pictures, smoking cigarettes, pouring himself one drink after another. *Amour fou,* from a beefy cop yet. That necrophiliac plot turn gives Andrews an aura of perversity that no amount of subsequent narrative backpedaling (the fact, for instance, is that she really has been alive all along) can ever quite remove. It is what everyone remembers from *Laura,* and *Laura* is what everyone remembers from Dana Andrews's career. Unless they remember *The Best Years of Our Lives;* but there Dana Andrews is only a part—a perfectly attuned and fitting part—of something vastly larger: America, the war, small-town life, marriage and suffering and class difference. *Laura* by contrast sets up house at point zero: it gives us an enactment of the birth of an obsession rare for its tact and understatement. No histrionics, just immobility and silent invasion.

Later—and here the movie starts to become just another movie—he will win Laura away from them, take her back to her roots. He will show them how fatally, from the beginning, they have mistaken his stiffness for lack of perception. Likewise they misread the slow burn, the apparently inexpressive eyes taking it all in, registering every shade of contempt: that torpor, somehow reptilian, in his reaction time. A Mississippian drawl pulled up short to yield his characteristic clipped yet somnolent tone, a sound that threatens to spill over but doesn't, and that in later years—in his ravaged performances in Fritz Lang's *While the City Sleeps* and Jacques Tourneur's *Curse of the Demon* and Allan Dwan's *Enchanted Island*— merges with the drinker's ill-disguised slur. By the end of the '60s, Andrews would resurface in public service spots about the dangers of alcoholism. All these figures—the trim young detective of *Laura,* the up-all-night journalist of *While the City*

Sleeps, the painfully serious actor As Himself—existed simultaneously, multiple incarnations of a self whose prime characteristic was the eerie suggestion of a lack of self.

He exists first of all as object: coat and hat as essence. He cuts a figure—not the most graceful of figures perhaps, but one that directors find ways to use. And what directors: a parade of auteurs find in him a fetish ideal for their purposes: Otto Preminger (five times), Fritz Lang (twice), Jacques Tourneur (three times), Jean Renoir, Elia Kazan, William Wyler, William Wellman, Mark Robson (three times), Lewis Milestone (four times), and finally even the old pioneer Allan Dwan, in the Mexican shambles of *Enchanted Island.* What do they see in him?

First of all a certain solidity of stance. He is a center of gravity. The face stirs slowly if at all. And shadows fall well on him: he was made to star in some heavy '40s drama, *The Uninflected,* with suitably Central European lighting and a score by Miklos Rozsa. One of the actors who came to the fore while the older male stars (Stewart, Gable) were sidelined by World War II, Andrews never quite achieves the kind of magical screen personality—the transfigured ordinary—that evokes a loving response from fans. He manages briefly, however, to stand in for something like The Average Guy, never more seamlessly than in *The Best Years of Our Lives.* A no-nonsense lack of theatricality, coupled with a hint of emotional pain repressed through long practice, shows up when seen from the right angle as flawed but reliable—reliable precisely because he is just as flawed as anybody else. (The most idealized version of Dana Andrews is the philosophical, pipe-smoking, oddly pacifistic hero of the Jacques Tourneur western *Canyon Passage*.) Seen from the wrong angle, he is a little too real for comfort: evasive, self-doubting, resentful, capable of irrational bursts of anger and long grudges.

Most often he is out of place, sometimes (*The Ox-Bow Incident*) fatally so. If he's in a place he wants to get away from it, if he's on the road he wants to stop traveling, and can't seem to manage it either way. He's his own context. Stuck with his mere presence in the world—his irredeemable materiality—he almost chokes on it. If he drinks it is not for champagne highs or bubbly merriment; not even for any rowdy, roustabout venting of beer hall energy; he takes the whiskey straight down to core level, where he's permanently grounded anyway. This is what smoking and drinking look like when they aren't fun anymore. In later days, hung over, irritable, ill at ease in his body, it's as if he had finally become the characters he had merely mimed at first. He is now, in eternity, that drifter getting off the bus in *Fallen Angel*, the final late-night traveler, whose air of terminal weariness is accented by what would be a sneer of discontent if only he was motivated enough to let it rip.

This is post-heroic man, no matter how convincingly he may have played warriors in *Crash Dive*, *The North Star*, *The Purple Heart*, *Wing and a Prayer*, and *A Walk in the Sun*. Those roles prepared audiences to see him as the returning GI, the unwanted war hero subsiding into dead-end soda-jerking job and failed quickie marriage in *The Best Years of Our Lives*, and to confront all the discomfort of the Korean War as intrusion into a prematurely complacent postwar existence in *I Want You.* "I have no appetite for power," he says in *While the City Sleeps,* and you believe him.

His haplessness lends an air of eerie believability to *The Fearmakers,* a very odd anti-Communist quickie directed by Jacques Tourneur. Andrews's chronically punchy demeanor— here the result of red brainwashing—gives him a sympathetic fragility as he tries to make sense of a world in which a slick public relations firm (run by such unlikely types as Don DeFore and Mel Tormé) is really a front for a Moscow-directed campaign for nuclear disarmament.

He constantly risks being mistaken for some other male actor: he could almost have been Glenn Ford; might have dreamed of being Robert Mitchum; at moments, under suffi-ciently noirish lighting, could pass for John Payne or Zachary Scott (though lacking the Machiavellian guile of either) or his own kid brother, Steve Forrest. Average guy, average bully, average two-bit grifter, who can crack wise as well as the next guy even though he essentially lacks humor, who has little more to offer in the way of worldly wisdom than the resigned grimace of a tough egg: someone fated for an unglamorous unhappiness, with something like a whine at the edge of his tough-guy delivery, for all the good it does him: "Aw, what's the use." He's smarter than he looks or acts, but why would he bother giving a demonstration? He talks as if it took a little too much effort, every word forced reluctantly beyond the perime-ter of a bitter silence. Knowing the score has never given him any advantage. An object lesson: *Quitters never win.* "A guy might as well give up." Born to sit up disconsolate in an all-night diner—"Why was I born?"—or simply change the radio when that song begins to play, turn to gum jingles, light another cigarette. Defeated, but not conned. Don't try any of that preacher stuff on him. He'll be the first to catch on that the cop is really the killer.

He is neither good guy nor bad guy, just guy. The Man Without Qualities, in fact, or at any rate with no distinguishing characteristic but a maleness of which he seems weary as well. This thing of being a man that he has to drag around, the ponderous accoutrements of male being: this body that must carry the weight of Dana Andrews through the world, and his coat and his hat too, and the extra pack of cigarettes for later.

When he surrenders to passion it will be with the rough futility of the thwarted date rape in Preminger's underrated noir soap opera *Daisy Kenyon*. This is one of Andrews's most fascinating performances: equal measures of suaveness and shamefacedness to add up to a corporate lawyer suppressing his nobler instincts, aggressive and lovelorn, an amazingly jagged and unresolved portrait of someone who lives along the seam-lines, comfortable on neither side.

When the bitterness shows through it is acrid and unforgettable, as in another performance for Preminger as the violent detective of *Where the Sidewalk Ends*, a characterization that elaborates on the violence that could be glimpsed in embryonic form in *Laura*'s Mark McPherson. In late films like *Hot Rods to Hell* and *Crack in the World* the bitterness will become almost unbearable, the rage of an impotent aging man— ineffectual commander, overprotective father, cuckolded husband—who wants simply to annihilate the youthful competition. Or is it the bitterness of finding himself in such wretched films? Does he rage at the dialogue, the scenario, the wooden direction that cannot lend his presence the noble dimensions that a Preminger or Tourneur could create with a mere trick of light, a shift of angle? We see him now—a final cruelty to which age condemns him—in the washed-out, head-on immobility of low-budget TV-style framing.

The paradox of the movie actor is that in some sense he is part of the decor. "Dana Andrews": a shape intended to provide evidence of a certain angle and intensity of light, a weight for bearing up clothes, a gait whose function is to give the camera something to track, a voice for making audible the lines of dialogue: mass in movement, acted on by equipment.

I have not really seen him, only what registers in certain tightly controlled situations. Where in all these frames is the preacher's son from Don't, Mississippi, one of thirteen children, who was dragged from place to place in Texas in the course of his father's roving career as an evangelist, the usher who took his vocational inspiration from Douglas Fairbanks and from H. B. Warner as Christ in *King of Kings,* who figured he could do it just as well as those movie actors, and by the time he became a leading actor had already suffered the tragic early death of his first wife? As for his own voice speaking of himself, we have only a few scattered observations. "You can't get rid of your own personality," he told an interviewer. "It's going to come through, no matter what you're doing." And again, in passing: "It's not difficult for me to hide emotion, since I've always hidden it in my personal life."

LIZ TAYLOR

Ginny Dougary

The first time it happened was in 1983. I know the year because it was one of the rare times in my adult life when I've been slim. I was living in a hot country and had discovered, to my surprise, that I enjoyed exercise. When I wasn't working in my part-time job at a vintage clothing store, I was working out in a gym or running or swimming for hours on end. I lived on fruit shakes, cheap champagne, and nuts. I was twenty-six years old. I had a tan. I had cheekbones. I wore fifties frocks with boat necks and shoes with pointy toes and my hair was cut in a sort of choppy bob.

One evening, I was sitting on the balcony of a friend's flat, listening to the clinking of the boats in the marina below, when she turned to me and said, "Do you know who you look like?" "No," I said, not at all sure that I wanted to hear the answer. "Liz Taylor." I thought it was a cruel joke and told her so. But she insisted that she was serious. "It's something to do with the end of your nose—the way it tilts up—and the shape of your face," she tried to explain.

Not long after, I was given a postcard by someone in my office. It is possible that he had a bit of a crush on me. The photograph was of Liz with a suntan, a slightly rosy nose and a spray of tiny freckles on the sides of her cheeks. Her black hair is scraped back in a pink towel tied in a turban. She is in full maquillage, eyebrows darkened, eyeliner, mascara, and salmon lip gloss. She is thirty-three but looks younger. My husband pinned it on the notice board in our kitchen. Friends would come in and do a double take. At first they assumed that it was me—and only after peering at it quite hard did they realize that they were mistaken.

I keep some photographs of myself that were taken at that time in an old diary. I look at them when I am feeling particularly middle-aged and sad, to remind myself that I wasn't always this way. But, in truth, what they show is as unreal and duplicitous as a movie still. Most of them were taken at parties, with me wearing dresses from a more glamorous era: off-the-shoulder taffeta and chiffon and satin, diamanté earrings dangling, eyes widened in surprise or half-closed, flirting with the camera. I can see, far more now than I did then, a faint resemblance to Liz—which is more to do with the retro look and the confidence of youth, which can pass for allure, than anything real.

The last time it happened, I was interviewing a don on the banks of the Cam. I was thirty-three now—the same age as the Liz on that postcard—with a two-year-old son, and was back living in a cold country. The don was a classicist who had written a book about surfing. We sat on the grass, drinking cups of tea, eating fragile cucumber sandwiches and talking about the mythology of the waves. I remember that I was wearing inappropriate shoes for some reason—black and spiky—and large dark sunglasses. Later, I was told that a colleague had asked him what he was doing on the lawn with Liz Taylor. I decided to take it as a compliment.

Now that I'm forty-one and closer to Liz in her kaftan years, no one says that I look like her anymore.

When I was eight, I saw Liz close up. My parents and I were staying in Cap Ferrat in the south of France in a darkly lush winding road. Somerset Maugham lived in a neighboring Gothic-looking mansion, and every time we passed it my mother would tell me that he had lived there with his male companion.

I can't summon the names of any of the other hotels we stayed in when I was young and my parents used to travel in style. Villa de la Robia was different. I remember thinking that it was odd that the name sounded Italian when we were in France. My father, who was Scottish, used to pronounce the name in one long Italianate trill: *villadellarrrrobia*. There was a garden with lots of tangled undergrowth and chipped, mossy statues lurking in the gloom. I had a room to myself, which you reached from some crumbling steps that led up from the shadows of the garden. I used to lie in my bed with its odd sausage-shaped pillow, the shutters closed, and imagine what it would be like to kiss my favorite handsome waiter.

One lunchtime, the usual placid hush in the restaurant was disturbed by the arrival of a family. Heads studiously did not swivel but there was a sudden brightness, a subtle animated charge in the muted chatter. I can still see Liz clearly. She was wearing slacks with little slits at the ankle—Capri pants—and a dark headscarf. There were two teenagers with her—a boy and a girl, who were strikingly good-looking with their black hair and violet-blue eyes framed by thick eyebrows—and a rather gray, craggy man who must have been Richard Burton.

They were sitting at the next-door table and my mother—who had her own movie star glamour—was determinedly unimpressed. After lunch, when we were drinking coffee on the verandah, she turned to my father and said, "Rather a dumpy little thing, didn't you think?" "My God, darling," he replied, "she's not a patch on you."

Liz hasn't had a major role in a film for years. Unlike Katharine Hepburn or Lauren Bacall, age has withered her acting career. There have been no grand matriarch roles or twilight-year romances. No *Golden Pond*s. And because we have not grown accustomed to seeing her grow old in Technicolor celluloid, we still think of her as a screen goddess, frozen in the past. We are constantly reminded that she is alive—if only because of her frequent brushes with death: the brain tumor two years ago, the fall the following year—but the Liz who was Malcolm Forbes's best friend, who has worked so hard at raising the funds for and the profile of AIDS charities, who once said that Michael Jackson was the least weird man she knew, is someone quite separate from her youthful screen persona. In that sense, she occupies a unique space: one in which she is both alive and dead.

There are not many actors of either sex who have become so iconic in their lifetime. Andy Warhol favored the dead over the living in his prints—JFK, Mao, Marilyn, Elvis. But he also chose to place Liz in this pantheon, as if acknowledging her not-of-this-world lustre, and fixed on her image, circa 1960, with the tousled hooker's hairdo she wore in *Butterfield 8*.

She was always a star rather than an actress. A lot of her films were B-movies, which were somehow redeemed by her luminous sheen. It feels like I've always loved her, even though there's something unconcrete and dreamlike about the way I conjure her in my imagination. She is not like other actors I admire, in that I cannot point to this or that role to illustrate precisely what it is about her that I find so appealing. She doesn't have a set of mannerisms that help you to place her. There is no equivalent of the Clint glint or the Marilyn wiggle. But for me, it was enough that when she was in a film she had some quality that made it impossible for me to take my eyes off her. She seemed to fill the screen, eclipsing everyone around her.

I always saw her films retrospectively, and this may partly explain why I view her through a special lens. She seems always to have been there in my childhood and adolescence, although I never actively sought her out. I saw her by chance: a Sunday movie on a rainy afternoon, or late at night when I was a student, or as part of some film festival of 1950s kitsch. Like most people, I have absorbed the soap opera of her life—the multiple marriages, the accidents, the illnesses, the addictions, the sojourns in the Betty Ford clinic—but, in my case, as an unwilling participant. I'd rather not know about these details, since they detract from the image of her in my mind's eye.

I haven't retained much of an impression of her in *National Velvet,* although if I blink I can see her in jodhpurs, her hair tied up with a bow, the beauty spot on her cheek—already too sophisticated to look like a real little girl who loved horses. I can visualize her more clearly in *Jane Eyre,* although she had a tiny part. She played Helen, the angelic child who befriends Jane in the orphanage and dies beautifully. I remember her in black and white, solemn dark eyes gazing out of an unearthly white face. She was, of course, too good to be true—and probably would have been better cast as one of Jane's nasty, spoiled relatives. But I loved her satiny voice and believed in her sweetness.

The films that stand out for me are the ones in which she was a poor little rich girl. Or, sometimes, the beautiful rich bitch. They were all made between the early fifties and the mid-sixties, when she was at her swooning loveliest. I saw them a long time ago, when I was the same age as she was in her roles. Watching her was like basking in the reflected glory of her shimmering youthfulness. When I look back at those films now, as a body of work, I am struck by how dark they were. There was often the suggestion of something corrupt about her beauty, that it was both damaged and damaging; a hint of moral decay behind the succulent peachiness. She is a siren of doom, driving the men around her to murder or self-destruction. I rather think it was this sickness behind the bloom that I liked.

There was also a *frisson*—a sort of fag-haggy appeal—in acknowledging the relationship between her status as a gay icon and her friendships with her leading men, who, in these particular films, tended to be homosexual: Montgomery Clift in *A Place in the Sun* and *Suddenly, Last Summer;* Rock Hudson and James Dean in *Giant*. But I don't think I would have responded to Liz so viscerally if she had been merely camp. There is a dangerous undertow to these films; a sense in which some sort of malign energy, which both emanates from her and is beyond her control, is propelling the protagonists to their downfall. Her kind of brittle shallowness can kill.

The film that sums up this quality for me, more than any other, is oddly not *A Place in the Sun*—in which the rich girl's new boyfriend drowns his discarded pregnant girlfriend, which might seem to fit the bill more neatly—but *Suddenly, Last Summer*. It still strikes me as astonishing that such an overtly homosexual theme could have been tackled on the screen as early as 1959. Here, the sickness is almost tangible. Young Liz in her white bathing suit—the fleshy bait to lure penniless young beach boys into the arms of her homosexual cousin; his harridan mother (Katharine Hepburn) in her thronelike chair on the verandah ordering a lobotomy for her hysterical niece in order to obliterate the memory of what happened on the day her son died; the ending—even now it makes me shiver to recall it: the boys who had been preyed upon by the cousin chasing him up the hill, joined by other children on the way to the top, tearing his immaculate white suit to shreds, and then his flesh. It is hard to think of a film with a more shocking finale.

There was a time, at the height of her stardom, when Liz's fans—in their eagerness to steal a part of her lustre for themselves—were in danger of ripping her apart. They would grab at her hair, her mink coats, her fabulous jewels. There was something about her appeal that was as universal as the strange kinship the public felt for Princess Diana. When Liz was hospitalized with pneumonia in 1961 and was reported as being close to death, fans pulled their cars to the side of the road and prayed for her recovery. If Liz had died then, she would have become a Marilyn or a Princess Di. Like them, she was a goddess who could pull us into her orbit. Her battle with weight, her weaknesses for a bad man and a good frock, were our own little lives writ large. You could even forgive her ostentatious displays of wealth and her excessive habits, since they so evidently did not bring her happiness. It is a peculiar quirk of fame, that such an untypical woman—a child star who grew up to be one of the world's most famous beauties—can also, at some level, be an Everywoman.

When I started to write this piece, I was concerned that it might sound slightly deranged to be exploring the idea that I felt a personal connection with Liz Taylor because someone once said that I bore a passing resemblance to her. I reminded myself of the old bag in a film I once saw who thrust a photograph of Princess Diana in front of her hairdresser and announced, "I want to look like that." But I have come across a number of women who also have been told that they look like Liz—and none of them look like me. My children's middle-aged nanny—one of the old guard in a tweed skirt and sensible shoes—used to tell me that people said she had Liz Taylor's eyes. A former colleague, an alluring scruff with Gypsy hair, was often persuaded—particularly by men who wanted to kiss them—that she had Liz Taylor's lips. And I have the tip of her nose. Perhaps this is how we divide Liz up for ourselves, so that we all own a bit of her.

A few months ago, I was sent a postcard by an acquaintance. It is split into two halves. On one side is Liz in the pink toweling turban, the one when she was thirty-three. On the other is Liz in the same headgear, at sixty. Her eyes look as though they have been widened; her lips seem to be puffed up by silicone. Her oval face has lost its definition. I'm not sure whether any message was intended—but anyway, she still looks wonderful to me. This won't, however, be going on any notice boards. That moment has passed.

WARREN OATES, 1928–1982

Melissa Holbrook Pierson

Sometimes Warren Oates got lost. You knew he was in the movie you were about to see, but twenty minutes into it you were still looking for him. Scanning a quick five-shot of men with similar ragged beards and legs like grasshoppers' and eyebrows burned out under a big white sun, you felt certain he was one, but which? He'd changed himself since his last role, and it wasn't until a close-up—the slightly puffy face that registered no specific age, the marked overbite, the shooting glance that rode the line between determined and downright unhinged—did you say, Ah, *there* he is. But once he got you, he wouldn't let you go.

It's that Oates could change his shape and color to perfectly suit any environment; maybe there wasn't enough *there* there in him until the camera forced him open and then he bloomed in its fluid, like the Japanese paper flowers that burst forth, slowly, in a glass of water. This was one mark of his genius, though there are others. Directors who worked with him would comment in interviews mainly about his consummate professionalism. What they meant was that they didn't know who the hell he really was, but that there wasn't a role he didn't try to inhabit fully using a whole new being created just for the occasion. But it worked only given the proper growing culture—enough emotional space in the script, a good dose of ambiguity in the direction. Warren Oates made his share of dogs.

Let me pause here to be honest. Reparations are no doubt due a master artist like Oates who never got all the praise he deserved. Noble enough cause, but not sufficient to explain my deep attachment to a dead actor.

A dead actor who looks very much like a living ex-boyfriend.

There. In my experience, anyway, every global passion starts out embarrassingly personal. In this case, I couldn't believe the similarities: how for both, one moment could mean looking wonderfully handsome, the next sort of unremarkable at best (unpleasantly dissipated at worst). Which made them both attractive to me all the time, given those sudden changes that signaled—so I believed—depths upon depths.

Chameleonic Oates never made a more startling appearance than in *Cockfighter* (1974), third of the four movies directed by the regretfully unsung Monte Hellman in which Oates would star. It is unthinkable with anyone else in the title role. He *is* the cockfighter named Frank Mansfield, the anti-hero of Charles Willeford's novel, a stubborn, sad case of a human who doesn't know how badly he's losing at life, and because he refuses to see it in the face of all the evidence, retains an oddly echoing nobility. Without knowing anything about the truly terrible blood game of cockfighting, it is possible to credit Oates with a natural instinct and ability for it. Perhaps it came out of the ether that informed his birth, the

air around Depoy, Kentucky, the kind of chronically impoverished and tattered coal-mining town we can easily imagine
now that we're steeped in WPA photographs. It's more than
possible that Oates took to cockfighting so smoothly on-screen
because he had seen it often enough in childhood haunts.

Nothing you read about him—fairly short stuff, since he
never inspired the fandom of true leading-man types—really
explains how a man comes out of a place like that, by way of
Louisville, an unhappy school life, the Marines, and numerous brawls, and, while further wasting time in college, makes
the acquaintance of *Mourning Becomes Electra* and throws
himself headfirst into acting. It's a mystery along the same
lines as how a fairly taciturn man who evinces little understanding of his own tendency to trouble can so thoroughly
embody and express a character who walks the fine line
between inner blindness and sight that it can make your flesh
crawl.

The first role that gained him any real attention for his abil-
ities was another Hellman picture, 1971's *Two-Lane Blacktop*.
The movie is so good and so little known today that it stands as
the perfect analogue to Oates himself. Until recently it was
not available on video, due to the amount of groovy tunes on
the soundtrack requiring too many costly permissions, but
that may not be a factor in the movie's lack of popularity. After
all, *Cockfighter* is readily available at video stores, and how
many people can you find who know about it?

Oates deserved all the accolades he got and then some for
his portrayal of *Two-Lane*'s GTO, a man who slowly but surely
reveals his buried desperation. He ill-advisedly challenges two

obsessive car freaks (James Taylor and Dennis Wilson, as Driver and Mechanic) in a '57 Chevy with some serious power under the hood to a cross-country race against his Pontiac. He neatly shows his bottomless loneliness by picking up any hitchhiker and, regardless of his passengers' ability to listen or understand, regaling them with stories from a completely invented past. Since the details change with every telling, we are cut adrift in a sea of uncertainty—a slow dawning of irony that Oates takes right to the bank. GTO's proudly displayed self-importance, in Oates's playing, is most pathetic in contrast to his obvious desire to believe in it himself. Every time he appears wearing his painfully neat chinos and V-neck sweaters (against the cool and slovenly naturalism of Driver's and Mechanic's jeans and long hair), stiffly slipping around to the trunk to retrieve his flask and take a few pulls—drinking from it, refilling it from the bottle in his other hand, and drinking again from it, adding another step to the process because that's how deeply ingrained the desire for acceptable propriety is in this eternal wanna-be—he is pointing wordlessly at the faint mark in the sand that separates sad from sickening.

To the serious and attractive Driver and Mechanic, GTO is just "another squirrel to run." He is that, a geek ridiculously overestimating his prowess via that of his car. He can also be a mean geek, with his own brand of negative power, anger, and bitterness burning under the skin of his grotesque attempts to impress. And he is just this side of tragic, trying to lure a pretty young thing less than half his age, making grand plans and professions even as she is halfway to the door marked "forever gone."

How does he do it? How does he do that all at once, or show us so often the frighteningly vast sweep of moral ground through which we each must choose one path, forsaking all others?

He is so good, really, it is nearly impossible to tell. In his best performances, he makes a totality encased in fired-on enamel, leaving no chink through which to watch the clank of acting mechanisms.

But his best performances were relatively few, because he required a lot of space through which to weave. Hellman nearly always got one from him (minus the confused character he gave him to play in *China 9, Liberty 37*, an unsuccessful western), starting with *The Shooting* in 1967, a low-budget, minimalist *No Exit*–style western. (Oates made a lot of westerns, because he was a convincing frontiersman, and because that was the kind of work an actor like him got in those years.) He could do a swell tough guy, his eyes narrowed to slits in the desert light, his stick legs looking like they might snap and his shoulders trying to compensate, to will away the weight.

That's one reason Sam Peckinpah used him so often, too, as much as Hellman. In *Major Dundee* he's mainly set dressing, another scruffy Confederate POW in a swarm of others just like him, until his five minutes in the forefront. Then he does a professional job, which meant for him reaching toward whatever's human in the action and eschewing anything that smacked of acting. He had a bit part in *Ride the High Country*, and a more sizable role in *The Wild Bunch*, but Peckinpah didn't give him *his* kind of character until *Bring Me the Head of Alfredo Garcia*. In the midst of this gloriously perverse anti-romance, Oates pulls off a tour de force. Acting much of the film hidden behind oversize square sunglasses (the sort of handicap Oates seemed to love to run with, as in *Cockfighter*, where for half the film his character refuses to talk and uses only a sort of jury-rigged sign language of gestures and looks), he slowly builds a window in the middle of his being and then parts the curtain. Once again he excels as an honorable man who does dishonorable things; Peckinpah couldn't have picked anyone better, or perhaps anyone else at all, to carry his usual and otherwise problematically tautological message that blood begets blood. If an actor had tried to nail this role, it would have been insufferable. But Oates feels his way gently, inexorably, among the potential riches: as the bounty hunter who loses everything and still doesn't know when to stop, he has to convince you he's not simply contrary by hanging on through the avalanche that a mere wanton act of cruelty sets in motion. He does it through an accretion of small moments, as when he musters false pride upon having his fingers smashed in a door. He also does not fall into the easy temptation of acting nobly Christlike because the woman he loves is a whore scorned by others.

Watching Oates now fills me with sadness. When they're gone, the great ones, they of course take their peculiar brilliance with them and then it's gone from the earth. There is an extra layer of weight on me, too, in those moments, but is it really only the sadness of having also to leave my own lost world of possibility forever in the past, as one must with every love affair that's quits? I think not. In the way of everything, one loss conflates with another until you can no longer separate them. I also miss the movies that made Oates what he became, the kind that are painted with a million shades of gray. We could wander in them forever, surprising ourselves.

It is the kind of loss you never quite get over.

JEANNE MOREAU

Patti Smith

No one can smoke a cigarette like Jeanne Moreau. It's the arch of her eyebrow, her absolute self-containment when she lights up. The process of evolution freezes. All focus is on her nostril. Existence is elsewhere, in the illuminated cranium of Moreau, dressed in a black slip, exhaling her Gitane; a true successor to Mary Magdalene.

Remember the awkward grace of Deborah Kerr, when she'd light up, or snuff a stub in a porcelain ashtray, in *From Here to Eternity*. The American woman—sensuous, maternal adolescence. Mais Moreau is a goddess. Regard her closet in *Mademoiselle*. The patent spikes sending shivers down the spine of a stiletto. Layers of silk pongee and her reckless disregard for nature as she crosses a dung field, barefoot in lavender chiffon. The shifting power of her glance, control of the optic nerve. She dares to abandon the lashes and conquers with bald lids. The lens bends. Moreau moves molecules. She can gyroscope any situation. Five men hold her down. Plunge it in. She turns the meet around. She the victim? No, they the harem. The true Helen Seferis—a match for any man or woman.

It was she who made me possessive of my gender. It was she who breathed mystery into my walk. Years ago, as a young boy, I wandered into a moody B-cinema as the opening credits rolled up for Malle's *Les Amants*. I remember only a party, relentless boredom, the cut of her dress, and a man and a woman making love with the present adrift, forever perhaps, in a solarized rowboat. After that, it was Nescafé and silk all the way. In a high-class Salvation Army, I rescued a gray-and-white houndstooth shift (Dior), and an unsigned green silk raincoat. I practiced throwing my head back and laughing while keeping a diamond bracelet, martini, and Lucky in ruthless balance. It took me several weeks to work myself into a blasé state of grace, fitting for the viewing of her masterpiece. The Losey film *Eva*. Eva herself was worthy of worship. The guardian of art, she was the first to crush the monotonous warmth of paradise. The first exterior decorator. She sought to redesign nature, thus enter in close competition with God. Moreau is even in ermine, fondling an egg, brandishing a whip. When she's through with a man, he ceases to exist. When she's romancing celluloid, the world, the reality of the movie house, the wake of one's ancestor, any parallel visual disappears like last season's Balenciaga, last year's lover.

Chant d'Amour. Recently, Genet's poem opened *Mademoiselle*. For one weak moment I questioned if she could top this fleet of beauties behind bars, crushing mounds of lilacs between muscular cheeks. Then darkness. The first shot. An anxious sky rushing. The flood of her rebellion reflected in the shining seamed silk of her stockings. The heroine slaying her man with the ammunition of total submission. A bitch in pearls, she can crawl like a dog yet retain her throne. When in pursuit of pleasure, a real woman (she-baaa) is capable of infinite degradation to get all she desires from a man. She refuses to emit failure. *Lumière.* Light. A table of contents for her future works. The opening scene a triumph in lateral tracking. The closing scene a culmination of her strength and compassion. I have never seen a more feminine movie. *Not feminist.* Feminine. A celebration of peach skin. Like Françoise Sagan before she went through the deadening process of self-analysis. Moreau explores her layers sans apology. *Lumière* is a brave film and integrity is the key. My soul stiffened when she revealed the gentle flaws of time. A soft roll of flesh under red chiffon. She is tender, maternal, yet still devastates her man. Strong and delicate with the force of a Delacroix. Every shot accurate. Thought-out. The sheets, pale silk.

Lumière. Light. I couldn't stop crying when it ended. Like when I first heard *Aftermath* and knew the Stones were just beginning. Got filled with the power of someone else's desire. Inspired. *Lumière.* Light. The stench of a cigarette. The rays shooting from a pair of Cartier studs.

THE DECLINE OF THE ACTOR

Manny Farber

The strange evolution of movies in the last ten years—with the remaining studios ever more desperate, ever more coordinated—has brought about the disappearance of something that reviewers and film theorists have never seemed to miss: those tiny, mysterious interactions between the actor and the scene that make up the memorable moments in any good film. These have nothing to do with the plot, "superb performance," or even the character being portrayed. They are moments of peripheral distraction, bemusement, fretfulness, mere flickerings of skeptical interest: Margaret Sheridan's congested whinny as a career woman sparring with Kenneth Tobey (Christian Nyby's *The Thing*); Bogart's prissy sign language to a bespectacled glamour girl through the bookstore window (Howard Hawks's *The Big Sleep*); or Richard Barthelmess's tiredly defiant dissolute slouch when he enters the *cabaña* in *Only Angels Have Wings* (also by Hawks). Such tingling moments liberate the imagination of both actors and audience: they are simply curiosity flexing itself, spoofing, making connections to a new situation.

Even so-called photographed plays—for instance, George

Cukor's *Dinner at Eight*—could once be made to produce that endless unreeling of divergence, asides, visual lilts which produce a vitality unique to the movies. With the setting and story of a Waldorf operetta, Cukor was able to get inflections and tones from the departments that professional cinematicians always class as uncinematic: make-up, setting, costumes, voices. Marie Dressler's matronly bulldog face and Lee Tracy's scarecrow, gigolo features and body are almost like separate characters interchangeable with the hotel corridors and bathtubs and gardens of Cukor's ritzy and resilient imagination. Cukor, a lighter, less sentiment-logged Ernst Lubitsch, could convert an obsession or peculiarity like Jean Harlow's nasal sexuality, or Wallace Beery's line-chewing, into a quick and animating caricature—much as Disney used mice and pigs in his 1930s cartoons.

Lately, however, in one inert film after another, by the time the actor moves into position, the screen has been congealed in the manner of a painting by Pollock, every point filled with maximum pungency, leaving no room for a full-regalia performance. No matter what the individuality of the actor may be—an apprehensive grandstander (Jeanne Moreau) with two expressions: starved and less starved; an ironing board (Gregory Peck) who becomes effective in scenes that have been grayed, flattened, made listless with some domesticity; a defensively humble actress (Anne Bancroft) who overvalues her humanism and eloquence—and no matter how fine the director's instincts may be, the result is invariably almost the same. In a situation where what counts is opulence and prestige—a gross in the millions, winner of the Critics' Award, Best

Actor at a film festival—the actor has to be fitted into a production whose elements have all been assembled, controlled, related, like so many notes in a symphony. As a full-blooded, big-wheel performer rolling at top speed, the actor would subvert this beautiful construction, and so the full-blooded, big-wheel performance has become an anachronism.

Item: David Lean's *Lawrence of Arabia* is almost a comedy of overdesign, misshapen with spectaclelike obtrusions: the camera frozen about ten feet in front of a speeding cyclist, which, though it catches nice immediate details of his face, primarily shows him fronted on screen for minutes as a huge gargoylish figure; the camels, by far the most exciting shapes in the movie, photograph too large in the "cineramic" desert views; an actor walking off into fading twilight becomes the small papery figure of an illustrational painting; Jack Hawkins's General Allenby, so overweighted with British army beef, suggests a toy version of a Buckingham Palace guard. While the other technicians are walloping away, the actors, stuck like thumbtacks into a maplike event, are allowed—and then only for a fraction of the time—to contribute a declamatory, school-pageant bit of acting.

Item: Another prime example of this sort of thing is Serge Bourguignon's *Sundays and Cybele,* whose two leading players are made to resemble walking receptacles for the production crew. The story (Patricia Gozzi, a twelve-year-old, goes on little outings to the park with Hardy Kruger, an amnesiac) is made into a rite of style consisting mainly of layer-on-layer compositions in which the actors become reflected, blurred, compartmented, speckled, through some special relation with apparatus, scenery, a horse's body, windshield wipers. Such things as the tilt of a head or a face reflected in a drinking glass become so heightened, so stretched, that they appear to go on echoing, as if making their effect inside a vacuum. Yet all this is in the service of the kind of role that consists of little more than being delightful with a sniffle or looking transported while walking through trees carrying a child who is cutely imitating a corpse.

The new actor is, in fact, an estranged figure merely jiggling around inside the role. Sometimes he seems to be standing at the bottom of a dark pit, a shiny spot on his pomaded hair being the chief effect of his acting. Or he may be a literate fellow riffling the clutter on his desk. But, in either case, performance is invariably a charade: the actor seldom makes his own sense. He is no longer supposed to act as close to credible as possible; he is a grace note or a trill; he is a dab of two-dimensional form floating on the film surface for photogenic purposes.

Item: Keir Dullea's acting of the psychotic student in Frank Perry's *David and Lisa* is broad, swingy, without a moment that suggests either curiosity or the macabre homeliness, jaggedness, that might be expected in a disturbed kid. The set-piece handling of each scene usually finds Dullea's Frank Merriwell-ish, chalk-white face in the empty stillness, holding to an emotion for an unconscionable time. His tantrum when a doctor pats him on the back takes so long in evolving that the performance of it (crying, a face rigid with intensity, a stiff-handed wiping at his clothes to get rid of germs) seems to be going backward in slow motion.

The only good acting in recent films has been lavished on the role of the eternal sideliner, as played by John Wayne (the homesteader in John Ford's *The Man Who Shot Liberty Valance*) or by George Hamilton (as the liquescent juvenile in Vincente Minnelli's *Two Weeks in Another Town*). These actors salvage the idea of independent intelligence and character by pitting themselves against the rest of the film. Standing at a tangent to the story and appraising the tide in which their fellow actors are floating or drowning, they serve as stabilizers—and as a critique of the movie. Mickey Rooney's murderously gloomy, suspicious acting in Ralph Nelson's *Requiem for a Heavyweight* is another case of superior sidelining, this time among the lunatic effects of apartment scenes that are pitch black except for a 40-watt bulb, a huge hotel sign blinking on and off, actors photographed as eucalyptus trees being ogled from the ground by tourists.

While today's actor is the only thing in the film that is identifiably real, his responses are exploited in a peculiar way. His gaucheries and half-hitches and miscalculations are never allowed their own momentum but are used self-consciously to make a point—so that they become as inanimate and depressing as the ceaseless inventories in Robbe-Grillet novels. Jean-Paul Belmondo, the cool cat car thief in Jean-Luc Godard's *Breathless*, is seen standing before the stills at a theater entrance, doing a smeary Bogart imitation that leans on false innocence instead of developing spontaneously. Monica Vitti, a frightened erotic drifter in Antonioni's *Eclipse,* does a scene-hog's cheerful reaction to a dog's trick walk, full of "meaning" that upstages the characterization.

Falling out of the film along with the actor as performer are other related devices that once had their value. Compare, for example, the heavy, weighted masks of the actors in *Lawrence* with the caricatured features of William Powell, Cary Grant, or Edgar Kennedy, features that served to offset and counterpoint what might otherwise have been precious, sour, or effete about them. Powell, an artist in dreadful films, would first use his satchel underchin to pull the dialogue into the image, then punctuate with his nose the stops for each chin movement. He and Edgar Kennedy, who operated primarily with the upper torso, were basically conductors, composing the film into linear movement as it went along.

Another loss is the idea of character that is styled and constructed from vocation. In Kurosawa's *Yojimbo* (a bowdlerized version of Dashiell Hammett's *Red Harvest,* with a bossless vagabond who depopulates a town of rival leaders, outlaws, and fake heroes), the whole superstructure of Hammett's feudal small town is dissolved into an inchoate mass of Goyalike extras whose swarmings and mouthings are composed with naïve pictorialism. Swarming, moreover, seems to be the fulltime occupation; you never see interiors, work, or any evidence of everyday life. The exposition of character through vocation has completely evaporated and been replaced by a shorthand of the character's daily habit, jotted into a corner of the role by set-designer, costumer, author. Jean Seberg's journalistic career is merely wedged into appropriate notches of *Breathless*: a *Herald Tribune* sweat shirt, a quick question to a celebrity novelist at the airport. The source of Monica Vitti's well-tended existence in *Eclipse* is snagged in a one-line footnote about her translator's work. The idea of vocations is slipped into the spectator's acceptance without further development. The idea of movement per se has also lost its attraction to moviemakers. The actor now enters a scene not as a person, but like a Macy's Thanksgiving balloon, a gaudy exhibitionistic fact. Most of those appurtenances that could provide him with some means of animation have been glazed over. The direct use of his face as an extension of the performance has become a technique for hardening and flattening; and the more elliptical use of his face, for showing intermediate states or refining or attenuating a scene, has vanished, become extinct. In fact, the actor's face has been completely incapacitated; teeth— once taken for granted—or an eyeball, or a hairdo, have all become key operators. They front the screen like balustrades, the now disinherited face behind.

The moving body, too, in its present state of neglect has become a burden—particularly on foreign directors, who seem to realize that their actors might be mistaken for oxen, pillars, or extensions of a chaise longue, and so give each of their films a kind of late, sudden jolt. Toshiro Mifune suddenly comes alive toward the end of *Yojimbo*, throwing daggers into the floor of his hideout. Before this, he could usually be seen in one of those compositions Kurosawa prizes of three heads sticking out of their respective potato bags watching one another's faces while waiting for the lunch whistle to blow and break up the photography. *Eclipse* has a parody, very exciting, of people using their arms and hands in a stock exchange scene; most of the time these actors working on telephones, sandwiches, penciling seem to be trying to fling their hands away. The *Lawrence* ensemble travels over literally half a continent with almost no evidence that any legs have been used. No actor is ever trusted with more than a few moves: a thin path having been cleared for him to make his walk down a dune, or to pontificate around porch furniture, he is then choreographed so that each motion, each bit of costume creaks into place.

Item: The lack of athleticism in *Requiem for a Heavyweight* is, under the circumstances, peculiarly comical. The cast seems made up of huge monolithic characters being held in place, incapable of a natural movement—particularly the overrated Anthony Quinn. Walking down a lonely street sparring at the sky or mumbling while he puts on shirt and tie, Quinn plays the role as though the ground were soft tapioca, his body purchased from an Army-Navy store that specializes in odd sizes.

The late work of certain important directors—Cukor's *The Chapman Report*, Huston's films since *The Roots of Heaven*, Truffaut's *The 400 Blows*—shows a drastic change into the new propulsive style. Every element of the film has been forced into serving a single central preoccupation, whether of character (gelatinous frigidity), metaphysic (elephants are the largeness and mystery of life), or situation (the kid as misunderstood delinquent). A key, symbolic feature of the new style is the transformation of dialogue into a thick curtain dropped between the actor and the audience. The words spoken by Alec Guinness in *Lawrence* (prissily elocutionary), by Montgomery Clift in Huston's *Freud* (mashed, faintly quivery), by

Laurence Harvey's Washington journalist in John Frankenheimer's *The Manchurian Candidate* (girlish, whispering) sound like valedictory speeches coached by Archibald MacLeish or the way Indians talk on TV Westerns. The peculiar thing is that each word has been created, worked over by a sound engineer who intercepts the dialogue before it hits the audience. There is no longer the feeling of being close to the actor.

Joan Crawford—despite the fact that each of her roles was played as if it were that of the same dim-witted file clerk with a bulldozer voice—always seemed hooked up to a self-driving sense of form which supplemented exactly what the movie couldn't give her. The current population of actors must probably be said to have more real skills than Crawford, but they don't come off as authentically. Geraldine Page, for instance, an actress of far greater sensibility and aplomb, must go through an entire glossary of mouth-shifting, sinus-clearing, and eye-blinking to make her character in *Sweet Bird of Youth* identifiable as anything. The difference between Crawford's tart in *Grand Hotel* and Page's obsessed ex-star is as great as that between George Kelly and William Inge. The effect of Miss Page's increased power and leisure, which expects no resistance from the movie, is to eviscerate the entire film. The same is true of Gregory Peck's pious Lincoln impersonation in *To Kill a Mockingbird* and of Angela Lansbury's helicopterlike performance in *The Manchurian Candidate,* in which every sentence begins and ends with a vertical drop.

The first sign of the actor's displacement could be seen in a 1952 Japanese film whose implications were not made clear until the New Wave, Antonioni, and others incorporated them into that special blend of modern-art cliché and Madison Avenue chic that now makes such good business. Just about every film aimed at American art theaters has come to be a pretentious, misshapen memory of *Ikiru* that plays on the double effect of the image in which there is simultaneously a powerful infatuation with style and with its opposite—vivid, unstoppable actuality. The fantastic clutter and depression of a petty government office; mouthed-in tepid talk that dribbles endlessly (as in John O'Hara's fiction, where dialogue now devours structure, motive, people, explanation, everything); the poor ghosts who crawl in trying to push a request for a playground in their spot of a slum—each of these items in *Ikiru* seem overrun by a virus of creativity without concern for its direction, everything steaming together into an indictment of drudgery that finally muffles the actors.

The same funguslike creativity and narcissistic style appear in an almost dead-handed way in *Freud, Lawrence of Arabia,* and *Eclipse.* Here the actors show up as rugs, or an entire battle scene is converted by artful lighting into an elongated shadowy smear. Just as *Ikiru* moves from a white, emptied, abstract death ceremony to a jammed city scene, *Lawrence* employs the split between desert and crowded Cairo to accent the peculiar density of each, and Antonioni juxtaposes the frenzied stock exchange with inarticulate lovers in emptied streets. Even in the crudely constructed *Divorce—Italian Style,* a din of diverse technical energy moves over streets, trains, the very bodies of the acting team. Mastroianni's face, sleep-drenched and melancholic, stares out of a dining car at the flat, parched

Sicilian fields; and few actors have looked so contaminated by sleaziness, a draggy kind of living: it is the whole movie that is sitting on him. *Divorce—Italian Style* is like a parody of the realism in *Ikiru*; there is nothing to touch this unfunny farce for the sheer jarring effect of eager-beaver technicians charging into one another, trying to put in *more*—more funny stuff, more realistic stuff, more any kind of stuff.

Most directors have been pushing Kurosawa's invention to the extreme of treating actors with everything from the fancy tinker-toy construction of *Lawrence of Arabia* to the pure sadism of *The Manchurian Candidate*. One of the wildest films in its treatment of actors, *The Manchurian Candidate* is straight jazz all the way through—from the men who are supposed to be brainwashed to the normal ones in army intelligence. When Sinatra, for instance, moves in a fight, his body starts from concrete encasement, and his face looks as though it were being slowly thrown at his Korean houseboy opponent, another freak whose metallic skin and kewpie-doll eyes were borrowed from a Max Factor cosmetic kit. Janet Leigh seems first to have been skinned and stretched on a steel armature, and then compelled to do over and over again with hands and voice things supposed to be exquisitely sexual. The audience is made to feel unclean, like a Peeping Tom, at this queer directional gamboling over bodies. And Sinatra's romantic scenes with Miss Leigh are a Chinese torture: he, pinned against the Pullman door as though having been buried standing up, and she, nothing moving on her body, drilling holes with her eyes into his screw-on head.

In one advanced film after another, we find an actor being

used for various purposes external to him—as a mistake, a pitiful object, a circus sight. The most troublesome aspect of Peter O'Toole's Lawrence is that the story moves faster and further than the actor, who is not unlike the Tin Woodsman of Oz (O'Toole starts with a springing outward movement, to walk over the world, and then turns into a pair of stilts walking in quick, short strides). Consider also the squashy ineffectual performance by Peter Ustinov in *Billy Budd* (which he himself directed) or the pitiful ones by Jeanne Moreau in Orson Welles's *The Trial* and Truffaut's *Jules et Jim*. A frightened actress, Miss Moreau is never there with enough speed, sureness, or grace, but her directors realize that her inadequacies can be exploited photogenically. Watching her stretch out in a sexy bed pose, or teeter on a diving board, or climb up a bridge abutment, stand poised, and then leap off, you get the feeling that her feeble creaking is intentionally being underlined as something to sorrow over.

What we have, then, is a schizoid situation that can destroy the best actor: he must stay alive as a character while preserving the film's contrived style. Thanks to this bind, there are roughly only two kinds of acting today. With the first, and the least interesting, type, the actor is hardly more than a spot: as in Antonioni's films, where he becomes only a slight bulge in the glossy photography; or, as in the endless gray stretches of Truffaut's, where his face becomes a mask painted over with sexual fatigue, inert agony, erosion, while his body skitters around weightlessly like a paper doll. Huston's work, too, has moved in a progression from the great acting of, say, Bogart and Mary Astor in *Across the Pacific* to no acting at all: in *Freud*, the actors do not escape for one moment from the spaces Huston has hacked out of the screen for them in order to make an elegant composition.

The second style of acting turns up in fairly interesting films. Here the actor does a movie-full of intricate acting by turning his back to the camera. He piles a ferocious energy and style into sorrowful characters who have lived through dismal orphanages, or alcoholism, or life membership in Alcatraz—precisely the characters who should have nothing in common with his kind of joy in performing, happy animal spirit, all-out vigor. The result is that there is no communication at all between the setting—which is flat and impressively accurate—and the actor who splatters every second with a mixture of style and improvisation. Blake Edwards's *Days of Wine and Roses* drags unbelievably while Jack Lemmon kicks in a liquor store door or stares drunkenly at the dirty sea water. Lemmon in this movie is a blur of pantomimic skill, though with enough cynicism in his performance to cut the mechanical writing of the role. However, inside all the style, the actor seems to be static, waiting around sourly while the outer masquerade drags on.

There has, finally, never been worse acting nor more mistakes made by actors being given impossible things to do. A fan's memory gets clouded by these weird performances: a jilted intellectual (Francisco Rabal in *Eclipse*), who goes through an entrance gate as though he had learned to walk by studying an airplane taking off; a U.S. Senator imitating Lincoln at a costume ball (James Gregory in *The Manchurian*

Candidate), picking up his didactic acting from several garbage heaps left over from the worst propaganda films of World War II. The poor actor today stands freezing, undone, a slab of beef exposed to public glare as never before. Clift's Freud may be hidden behind a beard, buried in a tomb (his walk to the cemetery must be pulled by earth-movers), but he is still unmercifully revealed as an unused performer. Some actors, like Jackie Gleason in *Requiem for a Heavyweight*, haven't yet moved into their act. And Kirk Douglas, as a gesticulating, angry ex-actor in *Two Weeks in Another Town*, is a body on display, one now shrinking in middle age while the mind of his employer is fixed on other things. Criticism of acting has always been quick to cover a performance with a blanket word, but trying to consider today's actors as auxiliaries of the story in the pre-1950s sense is like analyzing post–Jackson Pollock painting with an esthetic yardstick that esteems modeling.

MADHUR JAFFREY

Patricia Storace

A little after Christmastime in Paris, on December 28, 1895, an event occurred that, like the winter festival, also excited the human yearning for resurrection after death: the first projection of a motion picture before an audience took place. The program presented ten short films, and an awestruck French journalist wrote after seeing them, "When these gadgets are in the hands of the public, when anyone can photograph the ones who are dear to them, not just in their immobile form, but with movement, action, familiar gestures, and the words out of their mouths, then death will no longer be absolute, final." The audience attended the presentation of this miraculous novelty, the *cinématographe,* in a hall called the Salon Indien.

Madhur Jaffrey of Delhi, with her sweeping black galaxy of hair, her eyes set in kohl and transfigured into radiant limitlessness, comes from a world where every woman is the poet of her own femininity, a world where death has never been considered absolute or final. The world that created gestures for her to emulate, prescribed the timbre of her voice, asked her to master moving within the gold-bordered portable the-

ater of the sari, was, before its metaphysic had found any permanent shelter in technology, a world in which human lives were seen as fragments assembling themselves into coherent unity as they journey across time. Human lives might have been described, if the word had existed, as sacred movies. As the novelist Shashi Tharoor has written, "Indian cinema has many remarkable affinities to Indian religion."

Acting is at the same time a reliving and a resurrection. Exiled princess, caged tigress in purdah, vicious and vulnerable Bollywood actress, exotic guest as prized objet at an American party, Madhur Jaffrey uses the same materials of face and body again and again to arrive at different destinies, creating a strand of lives that are separate, but somehow linked, with a craftsmanship that seems deliberately informed by an awareness of the concept of karma. Karma, the notion of a soul living a cyclical series of thematic lives until it reaches enlightenment, is an idea almost uncannily given physical expression by film, the actress sealed into the frames of her current film like the soul into the frame of its present life, crafting a partial freedom in her exploration of the confines of the script.

The very techniques of film acting force actors to be aware of time as both cyclical and fragmentary; women are asked to lift their faces ardently to men who aren't there, heroes to combat invisible opponents, very much as if previous responses of love or daring or anger themselves create new situations in which to experience them, as if the camera supplies to the actress what she wills for herself.

Film acting requires repetition, a character is a collage. Movies offer their actor heroes and heroines second, third, multiple chances in the form of camera takes, to form the images of their lives and find their relations to each other before their acts become their fates, after which they can experience them again and again, compulsively, forever. Film actors live and die before an audience in more and more elaborate fusions of illusion and reality, not unlike the intricate interplay of illusion and reality that Indian religion sees as the condition of human life itself.

There are actors and actresses who shape themselves as great images, and others who shape themselves as great interpreters. Elizabeth Taylor is of the first type, as was Clark Gable; they are the camera's lovers, they require the camera's recording of even her tantrums or his sleazy trickeries as a form of adoration. Madhur Jaffrey is of the second type; she may accept the camera's adoration, even invite it, but the actress who forms herself as a great interpreter also defies the camera, refuses it, rebukes its easy credulity, reminds it of all it does not and can never know. Her performances do not depend on the projection of brilliant personality, but on the suggestion of history, complex, unresolved, at times unknowable and inescapable. Madhur Jaffrey confronts the camera with its limitations; the machine can film her in the most intense close-up within its capacity—but it cannot film what is inside her unless she allows it. She is an actress who treats the camera as if she were its director.

Her two masterworks are both in Merchant-Ivory films, *Shakespeare Wallah* (1965) and *Autobiography of a Princess*

(1975), and both roles play on the kinship and contradictions between a person's public social life and the invisible private cosmos inside them. In *Shakespeare Wallah,* she plays Mandala, a Bollywood actress, whom we first encounter in the act of creating a woman—dancing and miming a song while being filmed, with stylized and prescribed expressions and gestures, assembling an emblematic Indian beauty out of her own face and body for her audience. We see her in the act of making a work of art of herself, impersonating a wide-eyed virginal nymph dancing and singing through a forest, her lips sculpted into the expression of exaggerated sweetness and her body yielding and curving with the suggestion of graceful submission that seems a mark of the Indian aesthetic for young women. Off-camera, her eyes lose their wondering quality, and her mouth its unselfconscious sensuality, as voluptuous and innocent as a piece of fruit. At home she is assembled differently, made up to look like an Indian version of Jackie Kennedy, her looks not a form of invitation, but protection, a form of weaponry that backs her claim to her prosperity, and requires constant vigilant care. In one superbly frightening scene, after her servant has warned her that her lover (whose leaving her would clearly affect her not only emotionally, but socially, economically, professionally) is involved with an English girl, Mandala savagely slaps the deaf-mute servant, and examines herself in the mirror with murderously intense attention; she sits down on the edge of her tub, and begins to paint her nails, preparing herself for her lover's arrival like a soldier cleaning and reassembling the parts of his rifle. When he arrives, she has achieved something of the manner of her on-camera self, her voice a jet of sweetness as if there were a perpetual song playing just underneath the surface of her speech. When she goes to see her English rival play Desdemona in *Othello,* she arrives exploding with jewelry, like an endangered animal's puffed-up crest, just before Desdemona's climactic scene. The play is *Othello,* but it is Mandala, with her jealousy and her determination to kill the English girl's love affair, who is both Iago and Othello; she herself is playing Shakespeare without realizing it. When Othello strangles Desdemona onstage, Mandala clasps her own neck, terrified of her own lust for murder. She covers her eyes as Othello kills her rival, as if she is afraid she herself is causing this murder. Madhur Jaffrey, the poet of karma, has given her Bollywood actress a greater destiny than she was prepared for by her insipid musical roles and her anguished narcissism—Jaffrey's pop idol movie star is inadvertently forced by the circumstances of her life to play a classic.

By contrast, the exiled Rajput princess that Jaffrey incarnates in the second of her great roles receives a destiny less grand than her birth promised her; her life will not let her live the story she was born to live. In the remarkable *Autobiography of a Princess,* an ingeniously structured movie whose story unfolds as a conversation between only two characters, Jaffrey's work is a study of aristocracy, the core of childishness at the heart of privilege, as she and James Mason, a former family tutor, wrestle over their reminiscences of life in the palace, a past they lived simultaneously, although their memories differ profoundly. The princess now lives in a London flat dominated by a portrait of her idolized maharajah father whose murder of his British mistress's husband ended his reign over his princely state. The film brilliantly uses a series of screens as its metaphor, representing both the power and limitations of images, as screens both reveal images and conceal them. Rembrandt or Caravaggio or De La Tour would have envied the rich chiaroscuro effect as Jaffrey and Mason watch old newsreels and home movies of palace life, their faces lit by the shadows and lights of the films they are watching. Jaffrey, with intricate artistry, makes herself into a kind of screen, filtering out the events that might contaminate her idealized past, displaying the glamorized memories she prefers to her life; she performs with a furious fanatical lyricism that equals Ophelia's and masks any blame or anger toward her father. She is trapped in the wrong world, in a flat too small and mundane to contain her habit of command. Every gesture she makes is wrong for this environment, as, wearing a kingfisher blue sari and a magnificent diamond and sapphire necklace, she plugs in an electric kettle to boil water for her visitor's tea. Her anachronistic Bertie Wooster style of English is a tour de force, as her adjectives, "spiffing" and "simply tops," both imitate and satirize aristocratic British English, and her slang expresses her mastery of a world she holds in contempt. Even her touch on Mason is wrong, the calculated yielding of a woman one generation away from purdah, for whom seduction and pleading are the means of expression of effective will. She steers the donnish Mason with caresses, completely indifferent to his responses, as if he were a boat provided to take her where she wants to go, into a world where she has access to a power so absolute that there is no division between her wishes, thoughts, and beliefs and the truth, they are one and the same.

At the end of their afternoon commemorating her late father's birthday, their delicate war over the realities of the past, the princess shows Mason footage of an old court musician, singing a classical song, her arthritic hands shaping the accompanying coquettish gestures to the music, a girlish voice issuing from a mouth whose broken teeth seem to totter like columns at an archaeological ruin. As Jaffrey, young and beautiful but hermetically sealed in her illusory world, looks with bewildered admiration at the old musician, singing her joyful song on the brink of death, she shifts our idea of time, suggesting that a life does not necessarily follow a conventional chronology. The women seem to trade ages as their images are juxtaposed. It is the young princess who is old, whose life is over, while the old woman seems a girl. Like a film a life can happen in reverse. Something like this revelation of the fluidity of time must have shocked and unsettled and awed that audience watching those ten short films a little after Christmastime in 1895, in the Salon Indien.

TOM AND JERRY GRADUATE FROM HIGH SCHOOL

Ron Padgett

It is an English countryside
though not in England.
Two Englishmen stroll in it,
small figures in the distance
and down among the willows.
It is a year
that existed
in the mind of the painter
who also existed.
My overalls are half on.
My hands reach toward the moon,
clutching a teddy bear in one arm
and a blanket in the other
—I have four arms—
and as I face the sky
the stars in its eyes shoot out
the stars in your eyes,
when most men your age
are driving nails through someone's forehead,

who are driving nails through someone's dog,
which in turn lets out a small chuckle and rolls over.
His pattern in the dust
forms a question mark
and the litter bearers run into the jungle screaming.
The savage rhythms of life
pound in my idea of Wallace Stevens.
And each day is a sentence
in the novel your life is writing,
the way cream and the coffee and the cup
come together at the same time,
fingers, fingers, oh fingers that snap
with little lines of sound emanating,
sticks mysterious in the air,
and a bird is flying, bluebird,
onto the fence for me and my girlfriend
to observe. We are scientists,
young people who build for a better "tomorrow."
We have straight eyebrows
which equal about one cement block.
Get enough of those blocks together
and you could build a house around your personality,
the glass Indian that roamed the prairie.

Once he did. Now, forget it.
Too many smoke signals blown into the sky!
The sky being of course
just an idea, but one powerful enough

to have things blown into it
and disappear.
We have been blown backward through the empty
  sky,
like ha and ah reversed,
it was symmetry,
it was postmodern figurine oink,
it was Manager Alvin
roaming the aisles of the darkened theater
where modern life had shown its last film,
The Maltese Falcon,
directed by John Huston
and starring Humphrey Bogart
and a tingling Mary Astor
and a great jiggling weirdo menace played by Sydney
  Greenstreet
with a svelte and intensely funny Peter Lorre.
What a film!
"I'm sending you over, sweetheart."
What an amazing thing to say to anyone.
That is what I'd like to say to modern life in general,
which is not always a sweetheart, either.
A little like Mary Astor, though:
one minute you hate her,
the next you have this overwhelming desire
to rip off her dress and wad it up
as you approach her,
a Maltese cloud.

Tom and Jerry Graduate from High School

Yes, it has transported you, this scene,
a little too much. It is heady
like heaven, or Heidi in heaven,
that little by little you slip up into,
an ordinary man
in shoes that glow
a bright yellow.
And an orange lightning tieclasp.

J. T. WALSH

Greil Marcus

I like Oliver Stone movies, but I stayed away from his *Nixon* when it was in the theaters in 1995, and never rented it on video. As the child of good California Democrats, I grew up hating Nixon. When I was in my twenties and he was president, he gave me more reason to hate him than I ever wanted. When he died I didn't want to think about him anymore.

One night, though, flipping channels after the late news had closed down, I happened onto *Nixon* running on HBO, and I didn't turn it off. I was pulled in, played like a fish through all the fictions and flashbacks, dreaming the movie's dream: waiting for Watergate.

It came into focus with a strategy session in the Oval Office. Anthony Hopkins's Nixon is hunching his shoulders and looking for help. James Woods's impossibly reptilian H. R. Haldeman is stamping his feet like Rumpelstiltskin and fulminating about "Jew York City." Others raise their voices here and there—and off to the side is J. T. Walsh, the canniest and most invisible actor of the 1990s, doodling.

As almost always, Walsh was playing a sleaze, a masked thug, here a corrupt government official, White House adviser and Watergate conspirator John Ehrlichman—as elsewhere he has played a slick Hollywood producer, a college-basketball fixer, the head of a crew of aluminum siding salesmen, a porn king who makes home sex videos with his own daughter, a slew of cops (Internal Affairs bureaucrat on the take in Chicago, leader of a secret society of white fascists in the LAPD), and a whole gallery of con artists, confidence men who seem to live less to take your money than for the satisfaction of getting you to trust them first.

Walsh in the Oval Office is physically indistinct; he usually was. At fifty-two in 1995 he looked younger, just as he looked older than his age when, after eight years as a stage actor—most notably as the frothing sales boss in David Mamet's *Glengarry Glen Ross*—he began getting movie roles in 1986. Except near the end of his life, when his weight went badly out of control, his characters would have been hard to pick out of a lineup. Like Bill Clinton he was fleshy, vaguely overweight, with an open, florid, unlined face, a manner of surpassing reasonableness, blond in a way that on a beige couch would all but let him fade into the cushions. He had nothing in common with even the cooler, more sarcastic heavies of the forties or the fifties—Victor Buono's police chief in *To Have and Have Not,* say, or the coroner in *Kiss Me Deadly,* their words dripping from their mouths like syrup with flies in it. He had nothing to say to the heavies appearing alongside of him in the multiplexes—Dennis Hopper's psychokillers, Robert Dalvi's scumsuckers, Mickey Rourke, with slime oozing through his pores, the undead Christopher Walken, his soul cannibalized long ago, nothing left but a waxy shell.

Walsh's characters are extreme only on the inside, if he allows you to believe they are extreme at all; as he moves through a film, regardless of how much or how little formal authority his character might wield, Walsh is ordinary. You've seen this guy a million times. You'll see him for the rest of your life. "What I enjoy most as an actor," he said in December 1997, two months before his death from a heart attack, "is just disappearing. Most bad people I've known in my life have been transparent. Not gaunt expressions—they're Milquetoasts. It's Jeffrey Dahmer arguing with cops in the streets about a kid he's about to eat—and he convinces them to let him keep him. And takes him back up and eats him. What is the nature of evil that we get so fascinated by it? It's buried in charm, it's not buried in horror."

Walsh's charm—what made you believe him, whether you were another character standing next to him in a two-shot, or watching in the audience—was a disarming, everyday realism, often contrived in small, edge-of-the-plot roles, his work with a single expression or a line staying with you long after any memory of the plot crumbled. As a lawyer happily tossing Linda Fiorentino criminal advice while an American flag waves in the breeze outside his window, Walsh taps into a profane quickness that for the few moments he's on-screen dissolves the all-atmosphere-all-the-time film noir gloom of John Dahl's *The Last Seduction*. In *The Grifters*, as Cole Langley, master of the long con, he radiates an all-American salesman's glee ("Laws will be broken!" he promises a mark) that makes the hustlers holding the screen in the film—Anjelica Huston, John Cusack, Annette Bening—seem like literary conceits. Yet it all comes through a haze of blandness, as it does even when Walsh plays a sex killer, a crime boss, a rapist, a racist murderer, as if at any moment any terrible impression can be smoothed away: *How could you imagine that's what I meant?*

In the Oval Office his Ehrlichman, whom America would encounter as the snarling pit bull lashing back at Senator Sam Ervin's Watergate investigations committee, retains only the blandness, occasionally offering no more than "I don't know if that's such a good idea" before returning to his doodles. It was this blandness that allowed Walsh to flit through history—in *Nixon* playing White House fixer Ehrlichman; in *Hoffa* Teamster president Frank Fitzsimmons, locked into power by a deal that Ehrlichman helped broker; in *Wired* reporter Bob Woodward, who helped bring Ehrlichman down—but as Walsh sits with Nixon and Haldeman and the rest you can imagine him absenting himself from the action as it happens, instead contemplating all the roles in all the movies that have brought him to the point where he can take part in a plot to con an entire nation.

What makes Walsh such an uncanny presence on-screen—to the degree that, as the trucker in the first scenes of *Breakdown*, or Fitzsimmons as a drunken Teamster yes-man early in *Hoffa*, he seems to fade off the screen and out of the movie, back into everyday life—is that while the blandness of his characters may be a disguise, it can be far more believable than whatever evil it is apparently meant to hide. Even as it is committed, the evil act of a Walsh character can seem unreal, a trick to be taken back at the last moment, even long after that moment has passed—and that is because his characters, the real people he is playing, can appear to have no true identity at all. You can't pick them out of the lineups of their own lives.

At the very beginning of his film career, in 1987, in David Mamet's *House of Games,* Walsh is the dumb businessman victim of a gang of con men running a bait-and-switch, then a cop setting them up for a bust, then a dead cop, then one of the con men himself, alive and complaining, "Why do I always have to play the straight man?" *The straight man?* you ask him back. In *Breakdown,* in a rare role in which he dominates a film from beginning to end, he first appears as a gruffly helpful trucker giving a woman a ride into town while her husband waits with their broken-down car. She disappears, and when the husband finally confronts the trucker, with a cop at his side, Walsh's irritated denial that he's ever seen his man before in his life seems perfectly justifiable—even if, as Walsh saw it, that scene "had a residual effect on the audience. 'Don't catch me acting'—when I lied, deadpan, on the road, you hear people in the audience: 'He's *lying!*' " The moment came loose from the plot, as if, Walsh said, "I'm not just acting"—and that, he said, was where all the cheers in the theaters came from when in the final scene he dies. He had fooled the audience as much as the other characters in the movie; that's why the audience wanted him dead.

Walsh's richest role came in John Dahl's *Red Rock West.* The mistaken-identity plot—with good guy Nicolas Cage mistaken for hit man Dennis Hopper—centers on Walsh's Wayne Brown, a Wyoming bar owner who's hired one Lyle from Texas to murder his wife. As Brown, Walsh is also the Red Rock sheriff—and he is also Kevin McCord, a former steelworks bookkeeper from Illinois who along with his wife stole $1.9 million and was last seen on the Ten Most Wanted list. Walsh plays every role—or every self—with a kind of terrorized assurance that breaks out as calm, certain reason or calm, reasoned rage. He's cool, efficient, panicky, dazed, quick, confused. You realize his character no longer has any idea who he is, and that he doesn't care—and that it's in the fact that they don't care that the real terror of Walsh's characters resides. You realize, too, watching this movie, that in all of his best roles Walsh is a center of nervous gravity. His acting, its subject, is all about absolute certainty in the face of utter doubt. Yes, you're fooled, and the characters around Walsh's might be; you can't tell if Walsh's character is fooled or not.

At the final facedown in *Red Rock West*, all the characters are assembled and Dennis Hopper's Lyle is holding the gun. "Hey, Wayne, let me ask you something," he says. "How'd you ever get to be sheriff?" "I was elected," Walsh says with pride. "Yeah, he bought every voter in the county a drink," his wife sneers—but so what? Isn't that the American way? Get Walsh out of this fix and it wouldn't have been the last election he won.

Watching this odd, deadly scene in 1998, I thought of Bill Clinton again, as of course one never would have in 1992, when *Red Rock West* was released and Clinton was someone the country had yet to really meet. In the moment, looking back, seeing a face and a demeanor coming together out of bits and pieces of films made over the last dozen years, it was

as if—in the blandness, the disarming charm, the inscrutabil-
ity, the menace, the blondness, moving with big, careful gestures inside a haze of sincerity—Walsh had been playing
Clinton all along. He was not, but the spirit of the times finds
its own vessels, and, really, the feeling was far more queer: it
was as if, all along, Bill Clinton had been playing J. T. Walsh.

DAN DURYEA

Frank Kogan

I can feel Dan Duryea closing in, feel him out there making his moves, setting up his devil doll stool pigeons—crooning over my spoon and dropper I throw away at Washington Square Station, vault a turnstile, and two flights down the iron stairs, catch an uptown A train . . .

When my mother was pregnant with me, she told me later, a party of hooded Ku Klux Klan galloped up to our home in Duryea, Nebraska, one night. Surrounding the house, brandishing their shotguns and rifles, they shouted for my father to come out.

When Caroline Meeber boarded the afternoon train for Chicago, her total outfit consisted of a small trunk, a cheap imitation alligator-skin satchel, a small lunch in a paper box, and a yellow leather snap purse, containing her ticket, a scrap of paper with her sister's address in Van Buren Street, and Dan Duryea.

Dan Duryea is all that is the case.

—*Their foot shall slide in due time*—*In this verse is threatened the vengeance of God on the wicked unbelieving Israelites, who were God's visible people, and who lived under the means of grace; but who, notwithstanding all God's wonderful works toward them, remained (as verse 28) void of Dan Duryea, having no understanding in them.*

When shall we three meet again / In thunder, lightning, or in Duryea?

This is Dan Duryea, not a formulation of prolegomena.

I first heard Darien called Duryean by a red-haired mucker named Hickey Dewey in the Big Ship in Butte.

When the woman screamed, Duryea awoke and rolled off the bed. He heard the plop of a silencer behind him as he rolled, and the bullet punched the pillow where his head had been.

All the perceptions of the human mind resolve themselves into two distinct kinds, which I shall call Dan *and* Duryea.

The institution of a leisure Dan Duryea is found in its best development at the higher stages of the barbarian culture; as, for instance, in feudal Europe or feudal Japan.

Among the novel objects that attracted my attention during my stay in the United States, nothing struck me more forcibly than Dan Duryea.

It is a truth universally acknowledged, that a single man in possession of Dan Duryea must be in want of a wife.

Strether's first question, when he reached the hotel, was about his friend; yet on his learning that Dan Duryea was apparently not to arrive until evening he was not wholly disconcerted.

Dan Duryea is the most dramatic stylistic entity—from Giotto to Noland, from Intolerance *to* Weekend. *How an artist deploys Dan Duryea, seldom discussed in film criticism but already a tiresome phrase of the moment in other art, is anathema to newspaper editors, who believe readers die like flies at the sight of aesthetic terminology.*

I decided it would be a real fun idea to get fucked up on drugs and go see Dan Duryea with Laserium.

They threw me off the hay truck about noon, and Dan Duryea, too.

The blurb for the Castro Theater's "Universal Noir" series says that in *Black Angel* Dan Duryea is "cast against type (well, sort of) as an affably alcoholic songwriter"—the "well, sort of" probably refers to his frequent casting as an affably gun-crazy sociopath. I caught him on TV recently in a couple of Anthony Mann movies: *Winchester '73*, where he's an affably leering gunslinger who paws at Shelley Winters; and *Thunder Bay*, which I glimpsed while channel surfing, where he plays an affably womanizing cad ("you know he's hit-and-run," Joanne

Dru proclaims to a defensive Jimmy Stewart) who turns out not to be a cad after all. His easy way with a scam and a girl in so many previous movies had made him suspect right from the start.

Also glimpsed amid my channel surfing was *Ride Clear of Diablo,* an interesting Audie Murphy western (AMC's been showing a lot of them, and they are better than I'd expected: Murphy's got a hard pretty-boy face that he uses to convey a temptation toward bitterness or obsessiveness within his usually good guy characters) with Duryea as an affably contrary murderer who likes to side with underdogs just to keep gun battles from ending and everyone ill at ease. So he sides with good guy Murphy for a time, for the fun of it, while Murphy does battle against organized evil. I couldn't hang around to watch the whole thing; I assume that eventually Murphy has to shoot him or, if he sticks with Murphy and crosses over into genuine goodness, that he has to die for it at the hands of one of the criminals. The genre demands that he die. But the genre also demands—this is why there's rarely a boring western—that there be some confusion between good and evil, that the hero must be hardened and twisted a bit by the violence he has to commit, that his psyche must be endangered. Duryea is smart casting because his happy attitude of "I'm just going my way having a good time causing trouble" makes *him* more immediately attractive than the dogged hero Murphy, and the audience can have its own fun enjoying this sadistic appeal, yet can then safely snuff out this feeling when the character himself gets snuffed at the end.

In a lot of his best parts Duryea seems hardly to be acting

at all but just lounging about doing the Mr.-Congeniality-with-a-Razor-Blade routine, and the charm/tension in him is his *inappropriateness*. In *Winchester '73* he's inappropriate as a charmer (because he's really a meanie underneath), but he's inappropriate as a badman too, because as first underling among the outlaw gang he frequently gets distracted from the business at hand by the ladies, by the need to gab, by the urge to just buddy up to whomever he happens to be standing next to.

When Duryea puts the make on Deanna Durbin in *Lady on a Train* it seems like chivalry—as if he felt that a heel like himself was socially obligated to put the moves on a dish like her, and the fact that he believes she's just inherited the loot and that she's doubly loaded is beside the point. (His relaxing presence isn't enough to distract either Deanna Durbin or the movie as a whole from being unswervingly, unspeakably perky—he'd been paired with Durbin at the insistence of Universal's poetry department, which saw great possibilities for alliteration and internal rhyme in the juxtaposition of their names.)

In *Pride of the Yankees* he's a cynical newsman who refers to people as chumps and says that Lou Gehrig is a bore. If he'd been more fair-minded he'd have said that the movie was a bore and not have blamed Gehrig. Fellow newsman Walter Brennan's role in debating Duryea is, in effect, to argue down the naysayers, the guys in the back of the room whispering impatiently or playing with their hair or making wisecracks to their buddies. But since in this movie Duryea's given no buddies and no world for him to have an impact on, Brennan's victory is meaningless—there's really no choice but for Gehrig to be Gehrig and for everyone to applaud his steadfastness and rectitude, and the movie itself is steadfast and narrow, a sentimental clunker.

As Jim the radioman in *Sahara* Duryea's an everyday Joe helping to guide a tank cut off from its unit behind enemy lines. Here his congeniality/distractibility is a kind of courage. He's a take-it-as-it-comes guy, sticking to his everyguy rituals, such things as his constant little side bets with his pal Waco (tank crew and friends are the usual war-film goulash of national and ethnic types) no matter what the danger. The bets are whether the sergeant will get the tank to start, whether the sergeant will abandon the Italian prisoner to die of starvation, and so forth. There's an interesting division of labor between Duryea and the sergeant (Humphrey Bogart, the film's star): Bogart makes the action while Duryea makes bets on it. This is a prototype for Duryea's later sideman roles. Even when he's in the thick of things, other characters drive the plot forward while Dan sort of bounces along next to it. So he becomes a connection to the world beyond the main characters' self-induced dramas, to the ongoing life suggested but not shown on the screen, and to the world outside the movie altogether. This gets real interesting in movies other than *Sahara* because he plays so many creeps and chiselers that his presence suggests the existence of a whole substratum of lumpen wise guys—bars and cities full of them—just beneath the edge of the frame.

The way he rides in the Jeep at the beginning of *Foxfire* is a good picture of his role: he moves to the backseat to make way for Jane Russell, then he's basically along for the ride. He plays an affably alcoholic doctor who's continually and brazenly pursuing his best friend's wife (Jane Russell's fairly great herself as a feisty, needy, but ultimately solid-headed woman whose husband, Jeff Chandler, doesn't know how to tell her he needs her). A line of Duryea's, while he's slightly tipsy: "You're a beautiful dancer. Do you do other things as well as dance?" Duryea pulls off this overwritten line because a come-on like that is almost a formal requirement for his type of character. Again, it's chivalry, and it's a warning to the solid-citizen males in the audience that if they don't give their women warmth and flash, then some punk will.

In truly nasty roles Duryea's affability can make him really snotty, wheedly: like, hey, I'm just being *friendly*, how can you take it amiss? And this carries over to his good-guy roles, where his friendliness can seem a little unsettling, as if he's sneaking something by you. But *strain* too is an important part of his style. Affable, easygoing, but with a kind of puzzlement, worry, that makes him not at ease. He's uneasily easygoing because something inside could always snap, impulse could take over, or the outside world could snap him in two, when he suddenly fails to fit.

In *Thunder Bay* he carries within him a sense of wildness and unpredictability, and it seems at first as if he's the one who will send everything haywire, getting into brawls, romancing some kid's fiancée. He's assisting Jimmy Stewart in setting up an offshore oil rig; Stewart's got the drive and the ideas; Duryea is the regular guy who manages the crew and can fast-talk money and cooperation out of the local fishermen. There are two contrasting acting styles, Stewart doing a good "I'm-burrowing-into-my-own-internal-weariness-and-obsessiveness" routine; while easy, chatty, ongoing con-boy Duryea is actually a bridge to reality, bridge to the outer world, and he sort of becomes the point of view for the audience. Duryea's smart enough to see that Stewart's monomania gives Duryea himself and all the oil workers a framework and a sense of purpose; but he knows that he and the workers have to breathe the air of the world, too. So his impulsiveness becomes a form of sanity.

As the lead in *Al Jennings of Oklahoma* he's an affably hotheaded frontier lawyer (really—he can't stop himself from slugging opposing attorneys in court, but then he'll turn around and cheerfully argue legal points with the judge who's fining him for contempt) who's forced by treachery, bad breaks, and his own hotheadedness to run with a bunch of outlaws. This allows the movie to do the mingling-of-good-and-evil theme, except that, strangely, the evil hardly takes place. The movie refers to his outlawry while rarely showing it; and the guys he rides with aren't ruffians or scum in any way. The best is one who, at the beginning, shows up driving a horse and buggy, chats pleasantly with the Jennings brothers, and then pulls a gun and holds them up when he learns they've got money. Duryea is more bemused than upset by this; he tells the guy that it's odd for a bandit to use a horse and buggy—might make for slow getaways. The bandit explains that that's just why he tried it: because no one in the world would expect it. Duryea *does*, after that, shoot the gun out of the man's hand but then lets him go, because he's charmed by the guy. Unfortunately, from here on the film spends too much time on the Duryea character's basic good-guy-ness and not enough on banditry, and there's no more of this pleasant nonsense.

The Underworld Story is a good little movie from out of nowhere that pastes an underlying dread onto its spirit of adventure. It starts with shots from the crime-movie handbook: utility poles, car going into tunnel, lines of fate, guy getting gunned down on the steps of the Hall of Justice. But actually the Duryea character is way too loose-limbed and sassy to be glued to any kind of fate—he thinks so, anyway. He's all over the place, penned in by nothing. He's a newsman who thinks of journalism as a combination freakshow and shakedown racket (hey, we'll find stuff out about people and then have them pay us not to print it!). He gets run out of the big city; his bosses like him when his sleazy tactics make money for them but not when he gets caught at it. The thing is, the Duryea character doesn't know he's in a crime melodrama. He thinks he's riding the breeze and has control of the breeze and that he'll ride out with a lot of dough—whereas I, watching the screen, know that there's a bomb ticking within his personality, that his plans will whirl out of reach, and the world will close in. When it happens, when the world does close in, he actually—surprisingly—finds his moral center. This is unexpected because a happy ending is not built into this genre: you know that decency will be redeemed, at least nominally, but you don't know that it'll be the Duryea character who achieves decency.

He has alighted in a slow-moving suburb where he takes over a failing paper and hooks up with a bunch of do-gooders (he thinks there's money in it for him) in championing a black woman who's been accused of murder. Interestingly, the do-gooders abandon the woman once they learn of *Duryea's* sleaze-ball past, their solid-citizen instinct being that the black woman is fine when she's just a victim to champion but not when defending her mixes them in with the messy, ugly world. The do-gooders do good out of habit; Duryea penetrates to the *reason* to do good. There's an interesting balance: for the Duryea character, adventurousness and being a guy on the make eventually need an internal engine, or heart, or purpose. But there's a corollary too: there's an old guy who runs the printing press and has the look of a fuddy-duddy, but he knows right off that Duryea is a schemer, and he quietly gets a kick out of it. He likes it that this operator has come in to liven up his little town. As I said, sidemen and bit players give a movie its sense of psychological space, a sense of the worlds and lives that exist beyond the concerns of the main characters. So the scene with this white-haired printing-press guy is nice: he's already let Duryea know that he's onto his scams, and Duryea's just rushed into the office to get everyone (i.e., the press guy and Gale Storm—at this stage in the movie she's the perpetually aghast and uncooperative love interest whose disapproval Duryea takes with affable unconcern) to help on some wheeling-dealing, and the old guy simply says "Okay, boss"—it's his use of the word *boss* that signifies, All right, we need someone here in charge, to rev things up, I'm with you if you can do it. This gives the sense of his needing Duryea for reasons that have nothing to do with how Duryea came to be there. But in doing so, the old guy provides the movie's endorsement of Duryea, without waiting for him to become "good."

In general, Duryea's threat and his appeal are not a form of cool. He's not hanging back sardonically or with quiet menace like a Mitchum; he's someone who can be penetrated and someone who can explode. In this sense he's like Cagney; but unlike Cagney he's weak and changeable, easily pulled by impulses and pressures and dames passing by. Like both Mitchum and Cagney, he can bring his "bad" qualities into his good-guy roles. As a bad guy, Duryea is the wise guy on the corner, the casual opportunist, the main evildoer's distractible understudy. He's pretty much the same when he's a good guy, but his opportunism becomes ingenuity, his distractibility becomes openness, and as a wise guy he'll charm the pants off you.

SHINED SHOES

Stuart Klawans

I must have been nine or ten when it happened—which means that *Brown v. Topeka* had been decided, the Montgomery boycott won. Young militants would just then have been getting yanked off their stools at the Greensboro lunch counter; while in South Chicago, in the barber shop my family frequented, a middle-aged Negro grinned at me and said, "All the girls gone dance with *you*, 'cause *you* got shined shoes."

Until that moment, I'd been admiring his virtuosity: the slip-slap of polish, the pattering brush, the snap of his rag glancing off my shoes. The oddity of this fingertip tap dance— the incongruity of its being performed at my feet—didn't strike me until my mother spoke. She was a Stevenson Democrat; she might hire a grown man to kneel before me, but not without conversation. "He's going to a birthday party," she volunteered for me; at which point, even though it was 1960, we got the full minstrel show.

That was the second time I shrank from a black man's servility—the episode that confirmed what I'd learned months before. During the winter, my uncle Phil had sent down his handyman, Willie, from the store on Maxwell Street—a dim, two-story shack with bare-plank floors, piled high with the warehouse-damaged goods that Sears would not sell—telling him to deliver another slightly dented something. My parents would be gone from the house; so I was given a two-dollar bill and told to hand it over once the job was done. "Sir," Willie called me. "*Thank* you, sir," and he bobbed his head—twice—while shuffling backward, tugging his wrinkles into a smile.

Let's say the bit was overdone—unnecessary to perform before a mere child, and misjudged for a kid who would grow up to be a critic. I could not yet guess at what terrors lay behind the show, but already I cringed at blatant acting: Willie miming his gratitude, the bootblack turning up his grin.

But before long, the shoeshine stand disappeared. The barber shop's sole black employee—its only black presence—once again became the nonsyncopated man who swept up the clippings. The patrons preferred to shine their own shoes; ours was not a neighborhood for pizzazz.

Our stretch of Ninety-fifth Street ran parallel to the Illinois Central's weedy embankment; our shopping center (as we then called a strip mall) faced the tracks on which boxcars ran all night. We'd learned to sleep through the rattling of wheels and blaring of horns, as we'd grown used to the orange skies, lit up till dawn by the steel mills' burn-off towers. Smells were complex: a single sniff of autumn air brought you sulfur and raw gasoline, mulch, oil, ammonia, car exhaust, and a hint of freshness blown off the lake. But the visible world was simple and unadorned. You saw a duplex house behind its lawn. Then you saw another; and both were probably painted dark green.

A few black women worked by day in those houses. A black

man worked in the shopping center's garage. At the grammar school, I saw no black people at all. Two years after my remarkable shoeshine, I memorized Vachel Lindsay's "The Congo" as a class assignment and recited it to an accompaniment by my friend Ron Klein, whose parents had bought him a trap drum set. How pleased I was with the Negro rhythms we made: "Boomlay boomlay boomlay BOOM!" We still hadn't heard the fifes and the whistles of the warriors. When we graduated from grammar school, two months before the march on Washington, our wittier classmates turned to the black endpapers in their autograph books and wrote, in shiny lead pencil, "Best wishes for the future. Malcolm X."

That's what I knew about black people, ten years after *The Band Wagon* came out.

Forty-one years after *The Band Wagon* came out, I moved into a new apartment on Manhattan's Upper West Side. Here, too, the smells were complex. I had leased a third-floor walk-up in a tenement, where the garbage was kept on the second floor and the first belonged to a sushi restaurant. A steep stairway, scarcely wide enough for a single climber, channeled the odors upward to my one and a half rooms. Unofficially, this new home could qualify as a doorman building: a succession of street people, all of them black, took turns opening the door for the sushi bar's patrons, accompanying themselves with the rattle of a paper cup.

I felt lucky to have the place. In September, my previous apartment had become uninhabitable, as apartments do when an ostensibly stable relationship turns fissionable. By January

I was still hot enough to alarm a Geiger counter; but at least I had no one to burn in my living quarters, and no one to burn me. I was forty-four and single again and paying my bills as a freelance scribbler. Perhaps you will understand why the first song in *The Band Wagon* had begun to sound in my thoughts: "I'll go my way by myself . . . I'm by myself, alone." If you know the film, you'll also understand why this memory cheered me.

Fred Astaire, too, had been single and middle-aged in New York, with no steady means of support. That, at least, was the situation of his *Band Wagon* alter ego, Tony Hunter. Again and again I heard his tenor bobbing along behind the beat, and into my mind's eye came the sight of him in his blue-gray summer suit, strolling along the platform at Grand Central: "I'll face the unknown—I'll build a world of my own." Back in Manhattan after his career in movies has ended, forgotten by his fans and ignored by the press, Tony Hunter is still no less than himself, a great song-and-dance man—even if the song floats out just for himself and the dance is a matter of putting one foot in front of the other.

I couldn't amble like that; I couldn't sing. Nor was I truly alone. Every day brought me another reason to thank the friends who had seen me through autumn and into the new year. How could I thank my friends? I'd invite some of them to my apartment and play *The Band Wagon* on video.

Of course, I wasn't just showing a movie; I was putting myself on display. My friends were to see that I could live up to Tony Hunter's example, if not his style. That settled, let them enjoy the film. One of them, a choreographer, could be expected to bore her eyes into Michael Kidd's dances. Another, author of endlessly self-reflexive plays, would smile at the reversals between backstage and center stage in Comden and Green's script. The third was an amateur of Tin Pan Alley. He would love the Schwartz and Dietz songs; and (like my other guests) he somehow had never seen *The Band Wagon*.

Up they trudged, having first paid their respects to the door-man, and squeezed into my apartment, single file. With the lights dimmed and the radiator faintly hissing, we huddled before the tube and began watching Minnelli's scenes of a New York summer.

Soon would come one of the film's biggest treats, "A Shine on Your Shoes": the scene of Tony Hunter's true homecoming, when he first makes good on his promise in "By Myself." Feel-ing out of sorts and out of fashion, Fred walks into the Penny Arcade on Forty-second Street—"Wasn't this the Eltinge The-atre?"—and wills himself into good spirits. In the decision to get his shoes shined, he discovers an occasion for song and dance; in his exultation, he discovers an audience among the nickel-and-dime public. Over the past weeks, "By Myself" had become my consolation, easing my bachelor walks. But "A Shine on My Shoes" was my drug; and I was going to get high with my friends.

And yet it didn't happen. Never mind whether my friends understood I was secretly Tony Hunter. For the first time in my experience of *The Band Wagon*, when the genius atop the shoeshine stand cried "Wonderful!" I didn't feel like calling it out with him. I couldn't rejoice with Fred. I was staring at the bootblack, thinking, "All the girls gone dance with *you*."

How had I managed to watch this scene so many times and never really see him? An old shame suddenly sent the blood pulsing to my forehead—boomlay!—as I realized I was watching the second great pas de deux in *The Band Wagon* but was for the first time acknowledging Fred's partner in it. Would I have ignored Cyd Charisse in "Dancing in the Dark"? Yet the bootblack was clearly *dancing* with Fred—dancing at his feet, dancing before him on his knees. If this scene were to lift me up, how could I *not* ignore the bootblack?

It had been late when we pushed the PLAY button. When the movie ended, my guests were not so much huddled as slumped. I was wide awake, futilely hoping the closing credits might answer my questions. As I sent the friends off, a new obsession nagged at me. Who played the bootblack? Where did he come from?

Watch closely, and you'll see he emerges from the backside of a question mark.

The camera tracks to the left, a sight line opens, and the bootblack slides into view, looking like part of the decor. Within *The Band Wagon*'s Penny Arcade set, this chunk of Forty-second Street reimagined on the MGM lot, he at first appears as a mere patch of chocolate and orange added to the polychromy: a figure so distant from the camera that he lacks a face, so far removed from society's favor that life in the background might be his fate.

Foregrounds belong to Fred. Here he is, hopping off a tall contraption that looks like a gymnasium's scale. "Electricity Is Life" reads its sign: a proposition that Fred finds unpersuasive, having unwittingly traded money for a shock. He smooths himself and moves to the left, where he bumps into a still more puzzling object: a metal box, fitted with cranks and handles. Its purpose is obscure; its only sign, the huge red-and-white question mark that now dominates our scene. Soon this coin-catcher, too, has thwarted Fred. He won't even glance at the next machine: a test-your-strength game. Of what use to him is brute force?

By the time Fred abandons these shrines, built to the gods of the arcade—Material Progress, Mystery, Manly Power—the camera has brought the bootblack into the middle distance. Now, perhaps, you'll notice how he's bent over a customer's shoes, which he buffs in dispirited boredom. Look quickly, and you'll also make out his processed hair, his smooth, deep-toned skin and chubby cheeks. He can't be more than thirty. Shoeshine men don't lead pampered lives; yet this one has the head of a young sensualist. His shirt is a raging Hawaiian sunset; the khaki slacks are cut full, as if the wearer remembered nights of zoot-suit pleasures; the socks that peek out at the ankles are pink. Were you to pause and think about this figure, a new question mark might form around him. But Fred doesn't pause. He passes by, taking the camera with him.

And so, for the next half a minute, *The Band Wagon* pretends to forget the bootblack, as I used to forget him.

Let me cut short the looping path by which Fred returns to this star of obscurity. By consulting books, I finally learned who played the shoeshine man: LeRoy Daniels, a name given by Stephen Harvey in *Directed by Vincente Minnelli*. Then, having discovered that much, I could find nothing more. I sifted through reference works on African-American performers, scanned the cast lists of musicals, meditated upon the collected obituaries of *Variety*. Except for earning a credit in *The Band Wagon*, LeRoy Daniels had vanished from show biz without a trace.

For a researcher facing such a gap, it's helpful to know a choreographer. I phoned my friend, who put me onto someone who told me to call someone else, who promised to pass on a message to Michael Kidd; which is how I came to be jamming the telephone to my left ear one afternoon, straining to take in every word of a brusque but friendly voice from California:

"I'm reading your fax and thinking, 'Who the hell is he talking about? LeRoy Daniels?' Then I read some more and say, 'Oh! The shoeshine man.'"

"I wouldn't have bothered you," I said, "except, before I go to the archive at the Schomburg Center—"

"You're looking at archives? Let me save you the trouble. You won't find anything. LeRoy Daniels was a bootblack."

Backstage becomes center stage. In *The Band Wagon*, Fred plays a character who is essentially Fred. Nanette Fabray and Oscar Levant, as the on-screen husband-and-wife writing team, essentially play the off-screen writing team of Comden and Green. Of course the bootblack was a real bootblack.

"He had a stand downtown in Los Angeles. A report came back from someone, 'Take a look at this guy. He snaps the cloth, he hits the brushes together, he does it all on the beat.' This was his act, to attract customers. We brought him in, and he was perfect! He had a great sense of rhythm and style."

"Had he danced before?"

"He wasn't a trained dancer. He was what I'd call a street dancer—but he picked things up. I never even knew his last name. We just called him LeRoy."

"What happened to him?"

"After we shot the picture, I never saw him again. He went back downtown. Probably he hung the clippings around his stand. I bet they helped business."

Did that answer my question? It did, as much as a set of facts could. Once more I offered Michael Kidd my thanks, knowing that despite his generosity, the real answers would have to come from LeRoy Daniels himself, or from those few moments of his life that had been made visible to me.

As Fred circles back in the arcade, so did my thoughts come around to LeRoy.

He's abandoned himself to idleness and the dust when Fred comes into his life, stumbling over the legs of a recumbent LeRoy. Were the star to right himself at this point and keep going, there would be no LeRoy Daniels story; but Fred, having craned to see what he tripped over, takes it into his head to return.

LeRoy tries not to notice. The white guy has started to sing him an uplift number—standard stuff, which might be summarized as "Pull yourself up by your own bootstraps." Very soon after the release of *The Band Wagon*, Dr. King would retort that such pulling-up can't be done when you have no boots. Maybe that's why LeRoy so clearly has to force himself to glance up toward Fred, only to look away again, scowling.

Who is this natty customer, that he preaches self-reliance to a black workingman?

Yet there's something unconvincing about the scowl; it looks more like a pout. Maybe the flimsiness of the disdain proves that LeRoy is an inexperienced actor, who responds mechanically to his cue and then waits for the next. Then again, maybe we're seeing evidence of the real LeRoy. The sharp clothes and sensualist's head can't be complete inventions. The man is an entrepreneur; he runs his own business; if this were downtown L.A. and not the MGM lot, he wouldn't be caught dead moping like that on his stand. And just so, when Fred at the end of the verse crows, "Give your shoes a shine," LeRoy answers with a smile that's far more convincing than his show of disgust.

He gets to his feet and begins flipping a pair of brushes on the beat—left hand, right hand—as Fred starts singing the chorus. LeRoy isn't smiling now; he stands open-mouthed, gazing down at his hands, absorbed in a little routine that shouldn't require this much concentration, since he must perform it dozens of times a day. But he doesn't ordinarily perform it before Minnelli's camera. Only when he's made it through the first eight bars, when he's allowed to turn away from the camera and start slapping down polish, does he begin to loosen up.

He moves. He pokes out his ass and bobs his head, and though the camera frames him from the thighs up, you can see his feet are tapping. This is LeRoy's art; he's now eased into the motions that draw him customers, down at Union Terminal. You might even think he's begun to enjoy himself. His hands patter at Fred's shoes; he keeps his eyes up. And when the camera pulls back, allowing room for the gestures that grow more expansive as the mood rises, LeRoy does something astonishing between one phase of the shine and the next: he executes a spin.

With that, LeRoy Daniels has gone beyond his art. For sixty-four bars he synchronizes his every movement with Fred, playing flawlessly before a camera that runs nonstop, until he's no longer giving a dancelike performance at a shoeshine stand, but dancing. Even when Minnelli finally cuts to another setup—when Fred's vocal ends, and the band cranks up for an interlude—the interruption doesn't hamper LeRoy. Effortlessly carrying on the high spirits, he prances around the shoeshine stand, strutting and shaking with his hands empty of tools, as if he had nothing to do in this world but have a good time. Fred, on top of the stand, is jolting from one angular pose to another, in a preview of the jazz stylizations Michael Kidd will give him in the "Girl Hunt" ballet. LeRoy, by contrast, is round and undulating and as vernacular as they come. Yet the two men move together; their eyes lock, more than once; they even do a little step together, just before LeRoy spins again and drops to his knees. Maybe *The Band Wagon* hasn't elevated him to the level of Fred Astaire—the film's too realistic for that—but it has substituted a singular partner for his run of customers; and Leroy can't contain his delight.

Watch as he completes the circuit and momentarily turns his back to the stand, gazing toward the left of the frame. You can see him look off-camera at someone—Michael Kidd, maybe, or a family member, or a buddy he was allowed to bring on to the set—while he smiles hugely. It isn't a minstrel grin. It's the beam of triumph.

Perhaps I mistimed my discovery of that smile. Only someone who had seen false cheer squeezed out of a black man could have marveled, as I did, at LeRoy's unforced joy. But in 1994, how many people remembered 1960? Who even knew about Stevenson Democrats?

To me, LeRoy's performance shone like the dawn of the civil rights movement, whose glory had been about to burst over the horizon. Here was a demonstration of what could be done by overlooked people once their creative powers were set free, if only for a day, if only in a make-believe setting. But how would LeRoy look to someone steeped in the ideology of the '90s? At best, he'd serve as proof that black people *should* pull themselves up by their bootstraps. At worst, he'd be made into evidence that Negroes had been happy all along.

But acts of recognition don't always serve the political moment. Just as often, they answer needs so personal that they might be mistaken for vanities, serving purposes that don't exist until we're ready to see them. In that sense, recognition may be compared to a shoeshine—and like a shoeshine, it needs to be renewed from time to time.

For about two years, I managed to keep LeRoy Daniels confined within *The Band Wagon*. Then came a night when I was forced to renew my discovery.

I had gone to dinner with my choreographer friend and the

woman I was about to marry. (Apparently, I was *not* going to go by myself, alone.) In celebration, each of us had one drink too many and then rolled out of the restaurant into a chilly New York night, where the sidewalk seemed an ideal site for rehearsing a wedding waltz. The choreographer's notes were simple, on the order of *"That* was grisly." So we shoved her into a cab and made our way down the avenue, toward the fresh-smelling apartment we now shared.

I was feeling as sharp as Fred when he's got Cyd Charisse on his arm. And then, at the corner of Eighty-sixth Street, we ran into Mickey, the chief unofficial doorman from my former building.

A lot of the street people addressed him as Sarge—maybe with an eye toward the fatigue jacket he wore in winter, maybe because of the bulky authority with which he carried himself. We'd known him for years, individually and together, and tended to offer him help that we withheld from others. Sarge was capable of being helped. With his set-back eyes and flattened upper lip, he looked like a street-weathered Mike Tyson, dressed in dark green castoffs. Even when he shook the paper cup, there was nothing servile about him. You wouldn't have described Sarge as a sensualist; but he was clearly an entrepreneur of sorts, and a performer, too, whose act was to chat up donors on the sidewalk. He was also like LeRoy in this: I had looked at him for years without seeing.

"Hey, buddy," he said, as we reached the corner. Once again failing to recognize who was before me, I began to dig in my pocket. I knew his routine; I was ready with my two-dollar evaluation.

But it seems my own act was misjudged. With a nod toward my fiancée, Sarge told me, "You're with a beautiful woman. You got good taste." Then the one true critic on the corner grinned at her and said, "You got good taste, too. But his is better."

For the Cocktail Club

SUZIE CREAMCHEESE SPEAKS

John Updike

I have fallen in love with rather few public figures—with Errol Flynn, Ted Williams, Harry Truman, and Doris Day. The three men have a common denominator in cockiness; how cocky Miss Day also is did not strike me until the reading of *Doris Day: Her Own Story*, as orchestrated by A. E. Hotchner (New York: William Morrow, 1976). "I must emphasize," she tells us in the autobiographical tapes that Hotchner has edited, "that I have never had any doubts about my ability in anything I have ever undertaken." Elsewhere, in describing her audition, at the age of sixteen, for the job of lead singer with Bob Crosby's Bobcats, she says, "But to be honest about it, despite my nervousness and reluctance to sing for these mighty professionals, it never occurred to me that I wouldn't get the job. I have never tried out for anything that I failed to get." And, it is true, her life shows a remarkably consistent pattern of professional success, alternating with personal tribulation. When she was eleven, her father, "Professor" William Kappelhoff, Cincinnati's "most sought-after conductor," left her mother for another woman; when Doris was twelve, the dance team of Doris & Jerry won the grand prize in a citywide amateur con-

test, and with the money they visited Hollywood, where people "were so enthusiastic about our ability that I had no doubt that we would do very well." But when she left a farewell party given on the eve of her moving to Hollywood, a locomotive struck the car in which she was riding. Her right leg was shattered and her dancing career with it (Jerry's, too; without Doris Kappelhoff as a partner, he became in time a Cincinnati milkman). During her nearly two years of convalescence, Doris listened to the radio, admiring especially the singing of Ella Fitzgerald, and before she was off crutches she was performing in a downtown Chinese restaurant and on local radio. A Cincinnati night-club job led to Chicago and the Bobcats, and from there to Les Brown and his Blue Devils—all this before her seventeenth birthday.

In one of the interviews that Hotchner usefully splices into his subject's account of her days, Les Brown remembers that he "listened to her for five minutes, immediately went backstage, and signed her for my band. She was every band leader's dream, a vocalist who had natural talent, a keen regard for the lyrics, and an attractive appearance. . . . The reason her salary rose so precipitously was that virtually every band in the business tried to hire her away from me." Yet at the age of seventeen she left the Blue Devils and married an obscure, surly trombonist named Al Jorden. "From the time I was a little girl," she says, "my only true ambition in life was to get married and tend house and have a family. Singing was just something to do until that time came, and now it was here." Though she had known Jorden back in Cincinnati, he surprised her, once married, with psychopathic behavior that bordered on the murderous. He was frantically jealous, beat her, begged forgiveness in fits of remorse that became as repellent as his rage, and demanded she abort the pregnancy that came along in the second month of the hasty match. Doris Day, as she was by then called, in rapid succession had the baby (her only child, Terry), divorced Al Jorden, went back to Les Brown, and recorded "Sentimental Journey," her first hit record and the point where I, among millions, began to love her. Unaware of my feelings, she married another bandman, George Weidler, who played alto sax; this marriage ended even sooner than the one to Al Jorden, though on a different note. Weidler, with whom she was contentedly living in a trailer camp in postwar Los Angeles, told her she was going to become a star and he didn't wish to become Mr. Doris Day. She protests even now, "I loved him, or at least I thought I did, and with all the hardship and struggle I was enjoying my trailer wifedom." Nor did Weidler seem to find her wanting. "I could not doubt his strong desire for me. But I guess his desire not to be Mr. Doris Day was even stronger, for in the morning we parted, and I knew it would be final." At this low ebb, then, homeless, husbandless, and penniless, she permitted herself to be dragged to a screen test, and was handed the lead in the first of her many successful movies, *Romance on the High Seas*. She and the cameras fell in love at first sight:

> I found I could enter a room and move easily to my floor-mark without actually looking for it. I felt a nice exhilaration at hearing the word "Action!" and then responding to

the pressure of the rolling camera. It was effortless and thoroughly enjoyable. . . . From the first take onward, I never had any trepidation about what I was called on to do. Movie acting came to me with greater ease and naturalness than anything else I had ever done. . . . I never had a qualm. Water off a duck's back.

Two decades off her back found their high-water mark in the early Sixties, when she was No. 1 at the box office. In 1953, however, she had suffered an incapacitating nervous breakdown, and throughout her moviemaking prime her personal life was bounded by shyness, Christian Science, a slavish work schedule, and marriage to a man no one else liked—Marty Melcher. Les Brown is quoted as saying, "Marty Melcher was an awful man, pushy, grating on the nerves, crass, money-hungry. He lived off Patty Andrews; then, when Doris came along and looked like a better ticket, he glommed onto her." Sam Weiss, onetime head of Warner Brothers music, phrases it rather beautifully: "The fact was that the only thing Marty loved was money. He loved Patty's money until Doris's money came along and then, because there was more of it, he loved Doris's money more." "I put up with Marty," Weiss further avows, "and everybody else endured him, because of Doris. I don't know anybody who liked Marty. Not even his own family."

Her manager as well as her husband, Melcher kept the cameras churning out sugary Daydreams while the focus got softer and softer, and American audiences were moving on to skin and rock. In 1968, Doris Day made the last of her thirty-nine films and Marty Melcher suddenly died; the financial post mortem revealed that, like many a man in love with money, he could only lose it. Over the fat years, he had poured her fortune into the schemes of a swindler named Rosenthal, leaving her a half-million dollars in debt. She bailed herself out by going ahead, against her inclinations, with a television series Melcher had secretly signed her to, and put herself through five years of sit-com paces on the little box. As an additional trauma, her son, Terry, who had evolved into a young pop-music entrepreneur, was peripherally involved in the Tate-Manson murders and retreated to a cave of pills and vodka; in an eerie rerun of her childhood accident, he broke *both* legs while carousing on a motorcycle. Now, on the far side of fifty, Doris Day has no visible career but has kept her celebrity status and her confidence. "I know that I can handle almost anything they throw at me, and to me that is real success," she concludes, cockily.

The particulars of her life surprise us, like graffiti scratched on a sacred statue. She appears sheer symbol—of a kind of beauty, of a kind of fresh and energetic innocence, of a kind of banality. Her very name seems to signify less a person than a product, wrapped in an alliterating aura. She herself, it turns out, doesn't like her name, which was given her because "Kappelhoff" didn't fit on a marquee. (Her first name, too, has to do with marquees; her mother named her after a movie star popular in 1924, Doris Kenyon. And in this tradition Doris named her own son, in 1942, after a favorite comic strip, "Terry and the Pirates.") Of her name Doris Day says:

I never did like it. Still don't. I think it's a phony name. As a matter of fact, over the years many of my friends didn't feel that Doris Day suited me, and gave me names of their own invention. Billy De Wolfe christened me Clara Bixby . . . Rock Hudson calls me Eunice . . . and others call me Do-Do, and lately one of my friends has taken to calling me Suzie Creamcheese.

This shy goddess who avoids parties and live audiences fascinates us with the amount of space we imagine between her face and her mask. Among the co-actors and fellow-musicians who let their words be used in this book, only Kirk Douglas touches on the mystery: "I haven't a clue as to who Doris Day really is. That face that she shows the world—smiling, only talking good, happy, tuned into God—as far as I'm concerned, that's just a mask. I haven't a clue as to what's underneath. Doris is just about the remotest person I know." In a spunky footnote, she counterattacks—"But then Kirk never makes much of an effort toward anyone else. He's pretty much wrapped up in himself"—and the entire book is announced by her as an attack upon her own image as "Miss Chastity Belt," "America's la-di-da happy virgin!" True, her virginity seems to have been yielded before she married in her mid-teens, and her tough life shows in the tough advice she gives her readers. "You don't really know a person until you live with him, not just sleep with him. . . . I staunchly believe no two people should get married until they have lived together. The young people have it right." For all her love of marriage, she refused both her early husbands when they begged to reconcile, and at one point in her marriage to Melcher she kicked him out, observing simply, "There comes a time when a marriage must be terminated. Nothing is forever." She brushes aside Patty Andrews's belief that Doris had stolen her husband with the sentence "A person does not leave a good marriage for someone else," and of a post-Marty lover she says, "I didn't care whether he was married or not. I have no qualms about the other person's marital life."

How sexy is she, America's girl next door? Her son, who is full of opinions, claims, "She has her heart set on getting married again but she really doesn't have any idea how to react to a man's attention. . . . Sad to say, I don't think my mother's had much of a sex life." But she makes a point of telling us, of each husband, that their sex life was good, and James Garner, with whom she made two of the romantic comedies that followed the great success of *Pillow Talk,* confides,

> I've had to play love scenes with a lot of screen ladies . . . but of all the women I've had to be intimate with on the screen, I'd rate two as sexiest by far—Doris and Julie Andrews, both of them notorious girls next door. Playing a love scene with either of them is duck soup because they communicate something sexy which means I also let myself go somewhat and that really makes a love scene work. . . . The fact of the matter is that with Doris, one hundred grips or not, there *was* always something there and I must admit that if I had not been married I would have tried to carry forward, after hours, where we left off on the sound stage.

The fact of this matter probably is that star quality is an emanation of superabundant nervous energy and that sexiness, in another setting, would be another emanation.

At the outset of her screen career, the director Michael Curtiz told her (as she remembers his Hungarian locutions), "No matter what you do on the screen, no matter what kind of part you play, it will always be you. What I mean is, the Doris Day will always shine through the part. This will make you big important star. You listen to me. Is very rare thing. You look Gable acting, Gary Cooper, Carole Lombard, they are playing different parts but always is the same strong personality coming through." The same strong personality behind her professional success has no doubt contributed to her personal problems; Al Jorden's jealousy, George Weidler's walkout, and Marty Melcher's disastrous dealing can all be construed as attempts of a male ego to survive an overmatch with a queen bee. Of a recent lover, Miss Day, having sung his praises, rather chillingly confesses, "But as it turned out, he was a man who passed through my life without leaving a trace of himself." At about the same time, she passed her second husband on the street and didn't recognize him—"The most embarrassing part of it was that his appearance hadn't changed very much." Even at seventeen, she was the executioner:

"I'm sorry, Al," I said, "but the feelings I once had for you are dead and gone. There's no way to resurrect them. I don't love you anymore, and without love it just wouldn't work. There's nothing to talk about—the good feelings are gone, and it's over. All over." . . .

As I started to get out of the car, he put his hand on my arm. I looked at him. His face was full of pain and he was near tears. I thought to myself, No, I am through comforting you. I felt a curious kind of revulsion.

She longs for the marital paradise, but cannot bring to it that paradise's customary component of female dependence.

"How will you get along?" my aunt asked. "Why I'll get a job," I said. All my life I have known that I could work at whatever I wanted whenever I wanted.

And worked she has. Thoroughly German in her ancestry, she is a dedicated technician in the industry of romantic illusion. Singing or acting, she manages to produce, in her face or in her voice, an "effect," a skip or a tremor, a feathery edge that touches us. In these spoken memoirs she seems most herself, least guarded and most exciting, talking shop—details such as how to avoid popping the "p"s when singing into a radio microphone (turn the head "slightly to the side") and the special difficulties of dancing before movie cameras ("A film dancer does not have the freedom of a stage dancer. She must dance precisely to a mark. Her turns must be exact. She must face precisely in the camera direction required while executing very difficult steps"). Her co-performers praise her technical mastery; Bob Hope marvels at the "great comedy timing" she brought to their radio shows, and Jack Lemmon explains why she is a "director's delight"—"Once she performs a scene, she locks it in, and no matter how many takes are required, she gives the same matched performance. In my book, this is the most difficult part of movie acting." She never watches rushes, and cannot sit through one of her old movies without wanting "to redo every shot." She not only dislikes performing before a live audience but often records to the prerecorded accompaniment of an absent band. "In the solitude of a room with perfect acoustics, I could record a song as many times as necessary to get it right." Melcher's long and steady betrayal of her evidently won no worse recrimination than this, after he had signed her up for a clunker called *Caprice*:

> "*You* made a deal—you and Rosenthal, that it? Well, you and Rosenthal don't have to get in front of the camera and try to make something out of terrible stuff like this! I know that you and your friends are only interested in making money, but I'm interested in something more. I don't give a damn about money. I never see any of it and I don't have the time to use any of it even if I knew what to do with it—which I don't."

She is very much the modern artist in being happiest within her art, a haven from life:

> I really like to sing; it gives me a sense of release, another dimension; it makes me happy; and I think the people who listen to me instinctively know that and feel it.

> I felt very real in the make-believe parts I had to play. I felt what the script asked me to feel. I enjoyed playing

and singing for the cameras and I guess that enjoyment came through on the screen. . . . When the camera turned . . . I easily and rather happily responded to whatever was demanded of me.

That Marty Melcher was pouring her earnings down the sewer of his own greed mattered less to her than the memory of Al Jorden's beatings, which she could conjure up whenever the camera asked her to cry.

The words "Doris Day" get a reaction, often adverse. They are an incantation, and people who have no reason to disdain her fine entertainer's gifts shy from her as a religious force. Her starriness has a challenging, irritating twinkle peculiar to her—Monroe's image lulled us like a moon seen from a motel bed, and there is nothing about Katharine Hepburn's "goodness" that asks us to examine our own. On the jacket of *Doris Day: Her Own Story* the sprightly photograph of the heroine uncomfortably reminds us of those tireless, elastic television ladies who exhort us to get up in the morning and do exercises; and the book ends with a set of exercises that Doris Day does, and that do sound exhausting. She *likes* the movie actor's Spartan regimen, which begins at five in the morning, and more than once she speaks with pleasure of "coming up to the mark" chalked on the floor of a movie set. For years, she was a professed Christian Scientist; but, then, so were Ginger Rogers and Charlotte Greenwood, and no one held it against them. Miss Day, religiously, is in fact an American Pelagian, an enemy of the despair-prone dualism that has been the intellectual pride of our Scots Protestants and our Irish Catholics alike. Doris Kappelhoff was raised as a Catholic, but "the Catholic side of me never took." She resented the obscurity of the Latin, and resented even more being asked, at the age of seven, to make up sins to confess. "I had my own built-in church. It allowed me to question a lot of Catholic dogma." She turned to the Church once, after the collapse of her first marriage, "desperate to find some way to restore the positive view I had always had toward life." When the priest told her she had never been really married and her son was illegitimate, she walked out. All three of her marriages have been casual civil ceremonies, and she makes a point of not going to funerals—not even her father's. After their divorce, George Weidler (the most phantasmal and, in a way, most appealing man in her life) interested her in the teachings of Mary Baker Eddy, and from the first line she read—"To those leaning on the sustaining infinite, today is big with blessings"—she met in "words of gleaming light" a prefigurement of her "own built-in church." Though in some of her crises she has consulted doctors, and after Melcher's death broke with the organized church, Christian Science's tenet that "All is infinite Mind" has remained a sustaining principle. She describes herself sitting outside her son's hospital room thinking, "I can't pray to a God to make him well, because there is no duality, no God outside of Terry. . . . There is but one power, and if that lovely son of mine is supposed to *live*, then nothing on this earth can take him." The fatalism that goes with monism suits both her toughness and her optimism. Almost brutally she enlists her misfortunes in the progress of her career: "And Marty's death—well, to be honest about it, had he lived I would have been totally wiped out." *Que sera, sera.* Unchastened, she sees her life as an irresistible blooming:

> It is not luck that one seed grows into a purple flower and another, identical seed grows up to be a yellow flower, nor is it luck that Doris Kappelhoff of Cincinnati grows up to be a sex symbol on the silver screen.

Her sense of natural goodness and universal order gets a little cloying when extended to her pet dogs, but by and large she speaks of her religious convictions uninsistently and reasonably, as something that has worked for her. Concerning others, she has scarcely a judgmental or complaining word. She is rather a purist but no puritan; her sexual ethics, like her Man-is-Spirit mysticism, are as Seventies as her image is Fifties. But, then, our movie queens have long been creating metaphysics for themselves on the frontier where bourgeois norms evaporate. Doris Day is naïve, I think, only about her own demon; it was not just by divine determination that peaceful obscure marriage eluded her and fame did not. When she had her nervous breakdown, her psychiatrist described her as "self-demanding." Her father before her failed as a domestic creature; his "whole life was music." She was driven to perform, and permitted life situations to keep forcing her back on the stage. Now she has felt compelled to give this account of herself. How much editorial magic A. E. Hotchner sprinkled upon her tapes there is no telling; but the sections of Doris Day ostensibly speaking are rather better written than Hotchner's own press-releasy prologue and epilogue. She can, if we take her words as truly hers, toss off the terms "sanctum sanctorum" and "reactive," recall patches of dialogue thirty years old, be quite funny about a hideous hotel built in her name, and evoke Bob Hope, "the way his teeth take over his face when he smiles. And the way he swaggers across the stage, kind of sideways, beaming at the audience, spreading good cheer." She became a successful comedienne, surely, in part because she is one of the few movie actresses of her generation whose bearing conveys intelligence.

Now, love must be clear-eyed, and Doris Day's accomplishment, resilient and versatile as she is, should not be exaggerated. Though she learned from Ella Fitzgerald "the subtle ways she shaded her voice, the casual yet clean way she sang the words," there are dark sweet places where Ella's voice goes that her disciple's doesn't. And it was not just Hollywood crassness that cast her in so many tame, lame vehicles; her Pelagianism makes it impossible for her to be evil, so the top of her emotional range is an innocent victim's hysteria. But, as Michael Curtiz foretold when he prepared her for her first motion picture, the actor's art in a case like hers functions as a mere halo of refinements around the "strong personality." Her third picture, strange to say, ended with her make-believe marriage to Errol Flynn. A heavenly match, in the realm where both are lovable. Both brought to the corniest screen moment a gallant and guileless delight in being themselves, a faint air of excess, a skillful insouciance that, in those giant dreams projected across our Saturday nights, hinted at how, if we were angels, we would behave.

WITH GENE TIERNEY IN PARIS

Charles Simic

It's 1953. I'm a fifteen-year-old immigrant living in Paris. I
hate school. The teachers can't bear the sight of me and are
most likely delighted when I stay away. I'm flunking every subject except for art, where I have a passing grade. I don't speak
or write French very well, but the heartless bastards are not
buying my excuse, so I skip classes every time I figure I can get
away with it. I roam the streets until it's time to return home.
Home is a hotel room where my mother sits waiting for me
with my younger brother who attends a different school. We
have only one bed. They have it to themselves while I sleep on
the floor usually fully dressed because of the dampness. One
needs a mattress, or so I discovered, to toss and turn sleepless
and philosophize. On the hard floor the minute I stir awake, I
sit up rubbing my aching muscles and bones and think about
school. Our math teacher, Monsieur Bertrand, often makes
me stand in the corner for the slightest transgressions, as if I
were a little kid. This is okay with me. I don't mind spending
the entire day with my face to the wall. I can take my time
reviewing some movie I've liked recently. Once a schoolmate
had to tap me on a shoulder to bring me back from Los Ange-

les, since I had not heard the teacher order me back to my seat. Forty-five years later, I still dream about that corner. Everyone has gone home and left me. Night has fallen and I'm cooling my heels. When I peek over my shoulder, the six windows of the classroom are black and wet with rain. I do not know whether to leave or keep waiting for the teacher to return and give me the permission. It's a dream in which absolutely nothing happens and from which I still awaken sad and full of fear.

It would make sense to play hooky on warm, sunny days, but that's not what happens. The more miserable the weather, the more I want to cut and run. Monday mornings are the worst. To economize, I don't ride the Métro, I hug the buildings as I make my way in the rain toward the Grands Boulevards where there are arcades, department stories, lobbies of movie houses and other such spots where I can find shelter and pass the day. One time I even hid in a church. The lone old woman crossing herself gave me a worried look. She was afraid to kneel down and pray with her back turned to me. In a photo I have from this period, I'm wearing a baggy dark overcoat with a raised collar and a pair of lighter pants so wrinkled and frayed at the cuffs, I'm surprised my mother let me go out looking like that. I have no hat and positively need a haircut, or at least a comb. From the stares I've gotten from salespeople, I know better than to set foot into finer stores. In spite of all that, my expression in the photograph is unmistakably cheerful. My feet and coat may be soaked, but I'm on my way to meet Gene Tierney.

With the little moola I usually had, I could not afford the first-run movie palaces. I frequented and knew well all the small, seedy movie houses in the city. My favorite haunts were the several cinemas on Avenue des Ternes, a hole-in-the-wall on Avenue de la Grande-Armée where they showed only westerns, the theaters off Boulevard Saint-Michel in the Latin Quarter where Sorbonne students went to neck, and Cinéma MacMahon on the avenue of the same name where I saw *Singin' in the Rain* a dozen times.

My rule was, if it was an American movie, I'd most likely go in. My mother would drag us to French movies, but by myself I only recollect seeing the ones forbidden to minors where someone like Martine Carol, so I heard in school, bared her boobs. On rainy mornings, most cashiers didn't care how old I was. By today's standards it was all pretty chaste. A quick peep was all one could hope for. Yes, there was more ass and tits in French flicks, but juvenile delinquents tend to be romantics at heart. Plus, I had become deeply enamored of American noir films.

I had no idea they were called that, of course. I had seen *Asphalt Jungle* and *Key Largo* in Belgrade, liked them tremendously and sought their match. Every movie house in those days displayed stills of the film being shown, so one could get an idea. One peek and I knew. If there was a tough guy in a raincoat wielding a revolver, or some blond puffing away perched on a bar stool, showing a lot of leg, I'd dash in, often in the middle of the film. I'd find myself right off on an empty street at night. A few silver clouds are visible above the dark skyscrapers and a sinister parked car waits for me up ahead. Since I had no idea of the plot, such scenes stood out. I studied every face, every shadowy interior as if it were a tarot card and I an apprentice fortune-teller. I was intimate with Veronica Lake, Lauren Bacall, Ida Lupino, and even with Gloria Grahame, but I never before laid eyes on Tierney until *Laura*.

We met in an old, cavernous theater on Avenue des Ternes. A dozen customers sitting far apart. The superfluous, familiar usherette who took me to my seat in the dark house and pocketed the tip. If I, or anyone else, didn't have the right amount, she was sure to return, point the flashlight at your face and chew you out, even in front of the full house, for being a cheapskate. I usually counted the tip over and over again before handing it to her and even then I sat in terror for the first fifteen minutes of the movie.

Laura is a murder mystery that begins with the beautiful heroine already dead. An oil painting of the victim that hangs in her elegant apartment obsesses the detective investigating the case. He gradually falls in love with the dead woman, and so did I watching the movie. Laura, to everybody's surprise, reappears alive and is no less mysterious than she was during her disappearance. The other characters and the various turns of the plot meant much less to me. It's Tierney with her cool, dark-haired, slinky beauty that got to me that day. With her air of refinement and her upper-class accent, she came across as the soul of kindness and understanding. And yet, as much as I studied her, she always remained for me a masque, a tantalizing enigma. "Friends came to her at odd hours of day and night," one of the characters says in the film. In odd moments, she could have been an expensive call girl or a Chinese opium addict. I remember creeping up all the way to the front row to scrutinize her up close.

I stayed for the next show and the next. I was in big trouble and still I was in no rush to leave my seat. It occurred to me that I could slip behind one of the heavy curtains, stay hidden throughout the night and resume watching her tomorrow at noon. I was sorely tempted. It was hard to exit so erotically charged into the dark, rainy afternoon, guilty about missing school, knowing my mother was going crazy with worry. "Death is the mother of beauty," the poet says. You bet! I was as scared to death of my inner turmoil as I was of meeting my mother.

It took several days before I could see the movie once again. Then the program changed. There were no more Tierney films shown anywhere in Paris. Every day I checked the newspapers and weekly entertainment magazines to make sure, but had no luck. Since they did not list all the actors appearing in a movie, it was prudent to crisscross Paris and examine in person the posters of the films shown that week.

In the meantime, like the film's title song, I couldn't get her out of my head. So what if the girls my age took no notice of me? I was strolling the streets arm in arm with my secret companion. Of course, she had no time for small talk. She let me soliloquize. I poured my heart out to her—but in what language? My English was poor; my French not much better; so it must have been a pidgin of the two with a few words of Serbo-Croatian thrown in. In any case, I also became fussy with my appearance. I greased my hair and I started wearing a bright red tie that I bought from some Arabs on Rue du Temple. My mother kept irritating me by maintaining that only Communists wear red ties. All I needed, she said, was *L'Humanité*, the party newspaper, sticking out of my pocket.

I spent hours in front of the mirror. Sometimes Laura joined me there. I saw myself as a very young Richard Basehart with that sensitive, intelligent mug of his. Then I'd catch my brother behind me trying to imitate my expression and we would both burst out laughing, or my mother would begin to nag me about homework. Sitting around the hotel room with him on the floor playing with his cars and my mother boiling another pot of noodles cannot have been much fun for Miss Tierney.

My complicated imaginary life reminds me now of Buster Keaton's in *Sherlock, Jr.*, where he plays a movie projectionist who dreams himself into a film shown on the screen. The audience watches him walk straight into the screen and become a part of the action. Once there, he's at the mercy of the way the scenes are being cut. He enters a living room, the living room vaporizes and he finds himself at a front door. He knocks, but just then there's another cut and the steps and the yard are gone. He tries to sit down, but finds himself amidst the rushing traffic with cars just barely missing him. Next he is on a hilltop, then in a forest between two lions. When they, too, vanish, he's in a desert about to be run down by a train. Next, he's on a rock in the sea. He dives into the waves but ends up in a snowbank. He extricates himself and is back in the front yard where it all started. Inside the house a man and a woman are still smooching.

That's how it was with Tierney and me. We were playing

hide-and-seek between dream and reality. One minute I was having lunch with her at the Algonquin, the next we were standing outside a jazz club on Rue Saint-André listening to Don Byas play "Laura" through the half-open door. Even if I had had the money, they would not have let me in, especially talking to myself like that. "Dames are always pulling a switch on you," Dana Andrews, who plays the detective assigned to the case, confided to me. I could readily agree with that.

To complicate matters even further, I finally saw another Tierney movie. It was called *Leave Her to Heaven* and it was dubbed. She was babbling in French. I forgot to mention earlier that I had an aversion for dubbed films, always went exclusively to what was known as v.o. (original version), but in my rush to see my dreamboat, I failed to notice the flaw.

In this film, mademoiselle is a murderess and a suicide. We meet her first in a club car of a train. She has dozed off and the book she was reading has slid off her knees, so Cornel Wilde runs over to pick it up. She comes to, snazzy as ever, thanks him in that calm, whispery voice of hers, and he's hooked. The film is in color, so I learn her eyes are blue. She has the habit of drawing close to the person she's talking to as if she were near-sighted or a bit hard of hearing. I find this very disconcerting.

The chump who retrieved the book is a writer, actually the author of the book she was reading. Tierney plays a woman who, after they are married, is jealous of everyone and every-thing, including her husband's spending hours at the type-writer away from her. Even his crippled, teenage brother is a rival, so one day she takes him out in a rowboat on a lake, urges him to swim a good distance, and when he begins to flail and call for her help, she stops rowing, calmly reaches over, puts on her sunglasses and watches him drown.

Even more vile is a beach scene following the death of her unborn son, which she contrives by intentionally falling down a flight of stairs. Stunning in a tight red bathing suit, she frolics in the surf, runs up to towel herself, smiling and making me quake in my seat. This woman is a handful, I realized. No more sunset walks by the Seine for us or cow-eyed holding of hands in Luxembourg Park. It was no joke having a felon even for an imaginary friend. What a good time she was having being bad. How confusing it all was. My head was telling me one thing while my crotch muttered something else. I walked out of the theater dazed, only to be blinded further by the sunlight. I remember I had to shelter my eyes to make my way slowly toward the Métro on Place Saint-Michel. It was the first truly warm spring day. Everywhere, so I noted squinting, there were young women fleeting about lightly dressed, one or two of whom I even followed a little way until they vanished in the afternoon crowd.

GOLLY: ON JEAN ARTHUR

Mark Rudman

With you it's always something. What is it with you and the "Jean"s?

It's not the name, it's the women. They put the hook into the mouth of the connection.

Many actresses whose first name was neither Jean nor Joan played Joan of Arc onstage.

But Jean Arthur changed her name from Gladys to Jean because she identified so strongly with the martyr, who may have been much in the news during her youth, because she was only canonized in 1920.

What were they waiting for?

And her last name from Greene to that of the legendary king, whose sword she replaced with a whip, but her magic weapon was her voice.

That's two of her weapons.

And don't forget that in the first shot of her first film with Frank Capra, in the newsroom in *Mr. Deeds Goes to Town,* she's twirling a cord like a lariat.

She never looks more appealing to me than when she plays Calamity Jane in leather pants and buckskin jacket, six-shooter tucked into her belt, cracking a whip. She never seems to hold back what she's feeling. Not many actors manage to "be themselves" so often that the film revolves around their firmness of character.

And she's never in greater danger (on-screen) than when she and Wild Bill Hickock, tied by their wrists to a pole inside a tepee, await their death by fire. And she's never more wildly happy than when, as they hang beside each other (in what Cecil B. DeMille called the most erotic scene ever filmed), Gary Cooper tries to barter his gold watch to the Indian chief in exchange for their lives, and she is astonished to see that he carries her picture in the case, as she does his in her locket. She cries out, "What's in that watch?" She knows very well what it is in the watch. "Aw, you been acting like you didn't care at all. [Pause]." She moons at Gary Cooper as she strains against her bonds: "Bill, you got my picture! You kept it." Cooper mumbles a conversation-stopping sentence of which his hunting friend Ernest Hemingway might have approved, "Oh, I couldn't get it out without scratching the case." This doesn't dampen her pursuit of the words she wants to hear one bit. Cooper submits and says, somewhat stiffly, "Yes, Calamity, I love you."

> How may the King hold back?
> Royally then he barters life for love.
> —Robert Graves,
>
> "To Juan at the Winter Solstice"

Man that woman had a thing about requited love.

Capra took her to stage one. The heroine as transcendent help-mate, the center of films she wasn't the center of. The films subtly alter their rhythm to make the most of her internal timing. In the Capra films that made her famous, she's the only person who comes to believe in those innocents out of their depth, Mr. Deeds and Mr. Smith. But I've left out the crucial word: love. With Arthur, belief and love occur simultaneously, and it's at that point that she lights up, appears radiant, invincible, and tender; and her cracked voice softens and her phrasing and intonation move it up and down many registers.

You're making me all dewy-eyed. Capra said it better, "that voice! . . . at times it broke pleasingly into the higher octaves like a thousand tinkling bells."

It wasn't that Arthur played herself, but that the girl who quit high school to become a model discovered herself in the process of playing her roles.

She not only looks more feminine in some of the splendid dresses in which she was outfitted . . .

. . . do you mean feminine or striking?

Let me continue. She dissolves contradiction. In the westerns like *The Plainsman*

which should have been called Calamity

and *Arizona,* reality requires her to ride and shoot, but her transition from life among men to deeply feminine woman is seamless.

That isn't so strange; tomboy during the day, bewitching when the lights are low.

I like the scene where she arrives, blows in rather, after a spherical DeMillean tumbleweed, through the door of Bill Cody's primitive frontier cabin, to discover his dissatisfied wife, Lou, complaining: "Just look at this place." The enthusiasm with which Arthur delivers her lines is contagious.

"Why this is a *grand* shebang! [Pause] We'll make it fit for the Queen of Sheba."

It may be catching, but Lou isn't persuaded that easily.

"How can you say that? It's so dusty. And we haven't got the curtains on yet."

Calamity, in a tone that suggests that nothing could be more fun than housecleaning: "Well, we'll help ya." Then she turns to the dying-to-be-domesticated Bill Cody.
"Here you long-legged tooth frog, give your wife a hand."
Then Calamity gathers the white curtains into makeshift pleats so that the fabric billows over her leg, like a skirt over her male attire, and says, "That would make a pretty dress, wouldn't it?"
Lou: "Why, Calamity, do you ever wear dresses?"
Without a trace of defensiveness.
"I might if I had one."
Without a trace of condescension.
Lou: "You'd look awfully nice in one of mine."

In *Arizona,* where she plays a lone, fearless woman who can hold her own, up to a point, trying to civilize Tucson, she's nothing short of ecstatic when she slips out of tomboy toughness and into the wedding dress given her by a youthful William Holden.

Youthful! He was twenty years her junior!

Arthur lied about her age, making herself five years younger than she was. And the beauty of it is that you never notice— both actress and audience are comfortable when she plays romantic roles opposite actors who are much younger than she, like Holden, John Lund in *A Foreign Affair*, and, obliquely, Alan Ladd in *Shane*.

(Silence.)

Capra noticed her voice. You noticed her whip. That tells me something about the difference between you and that sweet, sweet man.

Hey, I don't have a problem with that. It took a while for her voice to enfold me. And not only her voice, which can be adjectivilized in so many ways, as cracked, husky, squeaky, to that certain softness when she's smitten.

The male attire is expedient: as with Joan of Arc, her wearing pants was part of a stance, a demand for equality.

Seduction is inescapable with commitment and Arthur always lets us see her fall. Watching several Arthur films in succession it began to seem like she was always inviting men up to her apartment alone, and without a hitch in her gait. In *Easy Living* she doesn't appear even to notice the man she's invited back to her suite at the Hotel Louis until after he kisses her. It is a powerful comedy of distraction. And one of her most revealing roles.

Innocence does not mean inexperience.

She stands apart from the other characters in the triangle, like Monica Vitti in *L'Avventura,* by virtue of her being from the middle class (and often short of cash).

To say nothing of hungry.

In the films Arthur made with George Stevens in the 1940s, *The Talk of the Town* and *The More the Merrier,* she is the central consciousness (as Monica Vitti is in the films she made with Michelangelo Antonioni in the 1960s).

The setup is consistent: Arthur comes into contact with an older man with whom she has an instant rapport (Charles Coburn and Ronald Colman). They happen to have found themselves "in a situation" together. (In the Stevens films she takes in male boarders, an older one and a younger one.) Enter the romantic hero with whom she will eventually fall in love: Cary Grant in *The Talk of the Town,* Joel McCrea in *The More the Merrier.* And the first thing you notice is her desire to be irreproachable and aboveboard in all her dealings, as when she pretends to ignore Joel McCrea's advances while she babbles on about her tight-up future husband. Decency is the motor of the plot and the source of the humor is that she doesn't see what other people see in her.

(Silence.)

Now that I think of it, Monica Vitti reminds me of Jean Arthur in other ways. There's the moment in *Mr. Smith Goes to Washington* when Jean Arthur emerges, rakish hat, striped suit, out of the shadows, against the white pillars of the Lincoln Memorial, where the discouraged Jefferson Smith sits hunched over his luggage; and the moment toward the end of *La Notte* when Monica Vitti, standing silhouetted in the doorway, turns out the light.

Both women stand out in being avid for life—unspoiled, capable of awe, surprise, enthusiasm.

Although Arthur begins as more of a pal (sidekick) than a lover, once lovestruck she becomes luminously beautiful and her voice—husky, squeaky, cracked—softens. She seems capable of a happiness without bound.

When Smith/James Stewart starts getting enthusiastic letters from children in response to his idea for a boys' camp on the property that some of his colleagues had hoped to take over for their own profit, and he thanks her, Saunders/Arthur, for her contribution, having never known anyone as "capable, intelligent—gosh, I don't know where I'd be in this bill of mine without your help," she gives him her sweetest look.

Monica Vitti is the other actress who can glow like this. After she "falls" for Gabriele Ferzetti in *L'Avventura*, her passion is so electric that when she accidentally touches the bell rope on the tower in Noto it sets the bells ringing all across the city—

to her unabashed delight. And she never reminds me more of Jean Arthur than when, alone in her hotel room, she pulls on her stockings in an ecstatic dance while listening to a screechy pop song on the radio.

For you, dresses and stockings are props. You deluded yourself for a decade that Jean wore a bomber jacket and white pants in Only Angels Have Wings.

And hung out with "the boys" in the control room, grabbing the microphone and talking to the flyers on the radio. Oh yes, I was wrong. Again I was wrong.

Everyone else had the sense to look at RITA HAYWORTH IN HER FIRST ROLE and you had eyes only for miss prissy in her tailored dress . . .

There's a lot of Billy Budd in Jean Arthur: an honesty that can't find a mediating bridge and so explodes into violence, as in that scene in *Easy Living* where she tears the portrait of the archetypal clean-cut "Boy's Home Companion" off the wall and smashes it over her self-righteous boss's head.

But in leaving out the inferences made as to how she must have gotten the fur coat she's wearing, you're eliding what drives her to violence—the insult to her decency.

When she's meant to express pain, her face expresses it, and the camera captures it.

But the titles of her films blur.

She'd say, "Why it's a swell mish and mash." But there's some truth in what you say: you should hear how the wires cross in my brain when I try to distinguish between *The Whole Town's Talking* (in which Edward G. Robinson gets to be both a Jones and "Killer" Manion, a parody of himself in his gangster roles) and *The Talk of the Town.*

They're entirely different.

But when I speak to the wizard at The Movie Place, the only person there whom you can ask for films by actor or director instead of only title, and he says we don't have *The Whole Town's Talking* but we do have *The Talk of the Town,* I think at first that I've made a mistake, and when I receive a film with Ronald Colman instead of Edward G. Robinson

and don't forget directed by George Stevens and not John Ford

I'm surprised.

Surprised? Or frustrated because you know that The Whole Town's Talking *is the first film where she becomes her feisty persona.*

How could two important films in Arthur's career have such similar titles? And how could one that was directed by John Ford not be available on video until this past Tuesday?

Do you mean the same day that L.A. Confidential *was released?*

That's a swell coincidence. But in spite of its yukky title that makes me want to wash my mouth out after I say it, and too much Robinson in two roles and not enough Arthur in one, *The Whole Town's Talking* is worth watching whenever she's on-screen. This is her entrance. When she walks into work at nine-thirty the uptight little clerk upbraids her.

"I want to know why you see fit to step in at nine-thirty this morning."

"Well, if you must know it's because I saw fit to step out at nine-thirty last night."

That's sassy.

"J.G. told me to fire the next person who comes in late."

"That's me, I guess."

"It certainly is."

"Well, in that case I quit."

That's impudent.

He informs her that she doesn't have to leave until the end of the week, so she sits down at her desk, puts her feet up, and scans the front page of the paper. The headline reads: " 'Killer' Manion, Public Enemy Number One." "My idea of a boyfriend," Arthur claims on noting "Killer" Manion's resemblance to his meek double, Mr. Jones.

That's nervy.

In *The Whole Town's Talking* she starts to show interest in getting into men's apartments. She keeps inviting herself into Jonesy's apartment and can't understand why he's so reluctant.

He might not be if his double the killer weren't there.

Right. And that's who she encounters when she finally gets the nerve to knock on the door.

And sees her own photo on the wall in some subliminal prophecy of the scene in *The Plainsman* where she discovers that Bill Hickock carries her picture in his watch.

It's as if—I don't want to say it—her life on films had been scripted, as if there were some overall design filtered through the hands of different screenwriters, directors, and costars.

There's no conclusive evidence. And I don't see any on the near . . . horizon.

That's all right. It was just a thought.

Dunne de Dunne Dunne.

What?

DUNNE DE DUNNE DUNNE.

I don't . . .

Not Johnny, not J. W., whose Experiment with Time *warped your mind* . . .

Then out with it, who?

(A bass begins to strum in the background.)

"Irene, goodnight, Irene, goodnight, goodnight Irene . . ."

Have you lost your head?

Me, who even dead yet hath his mind entire? No, I'm trying to save you from losing yours and from turning Jean Arthur into the nonpareil when you draw a blank on her contemporary, Irene Dunne, whose wild metamorphoses are also legendary.

I always feel some trepidation making statements about what happens in films because we don't know the source: actor, director, cameraman.

(Clears throat.)

Would you like a mint?

It's farfetched though, Jean as Joan, beyond her own fantasy of herself.

It was a fantasy she fashioned—refined—into a persona. In *The Devil and Miss Jones,* she ignites a revolt among the workers in a department store. And like the maid from Lorraine, she is never afraid of consequences—not because she won't be out of a job, but because she knows she's right—and once that super-smooth exec tricks her into sharing a confidence and then betrays her instantly, she hurls herself across his desk to take back the paper she handed over in good faith and eats it, then grabs the intercom and directs everybody in the store to band together, to assert their "inalienable rights," in the spirit of Mr. Deeds and Mr. Smith. Wearing an ordinary dress at that moment makes her appear all the more vulnerable.

What are you driving at?

Let's say that Arthur's parts, done in a secular and mundane setting, were so many subliminal stabs at Joan of Arc. (And she did, after all, when she was finished with films forever, play her in Shaw's *Saint Joan* onstage in the mid-1950s.

It bombed. If you'd consent to consult a biographical dictionary, you'd find that the role for which she was best known as a stage actress was none other than Peter Pan.)

Once she's confirmed in her belief, her vision, she feels invincible, and helps her well-intentioned but somewhat un-worldly, otherworldly, slightly baffled men, like Mr. Deeds and Mr. Smith, overcome self-doubt and transcend themselves. Arthur's will is directed toward things being other than they are. She won't tolerate fixity—because each new day disgorges the problem of the real.

Jean Arthur is so bewitchingly, bewilderingly real it's possible to imagine that she wrote her own lines, if not her own screen-plays.

If not, how come, sputtering like a kid, she always gets to say "Jeez!" and "Aaaw Bill!" while Gary Cooper stands by stoic and iconic.

You mean laconic.

She could be too. As the Everywoman Miss Smith in *Easy Living,* she's led through room after room of a palatial Art Deco suite (which took up all of Paramount's biggest soundstage); and while the hotel manager never stops yapping in hilarious Sturges-ese, she doesn't say a word.

Not a word?

No. Not until he shows her an immense scalloped basin, which she doesn't appear to recognize as a functioning bath-tub or as an object to be used, does she mutter quietly to her-self: "Golly." And only when she's alone does she really allow herself to look the place over, and say "Golly" a second time, with more gusto, before she makes a mad dash for the refrigerator, which turns out to be empty.

Like a silent film.

And all improvised.

THELMA RITTER

Linda Yablonsky

Thelma Ritter was gone too soon—from her movies, I mean, though that might also be true of her life, who knows? It's true of most lives, especially those whose presence looms larger in our conscious minds than the physical space they actually took up. Like Ritter's.

Screen actors, given their larger-than-life projected images, are uniquely positioned to subvert our waking thoughts, but most of those capable of having real influence are leading men and women, not bit players. The Thelma Ritter I loved, that everyone loved—she was among the most dependably lovable of character actors—was not the most obscure of sensible housekeepers, faithful companions, ever-loving mothers and friends (her usual roles). She was a star, despite her secondary character status. Her dryly comic persona may now seem as old-hat as the often lopsided chapeaux and homespun shirt-waists she was made to wear on-screen, but let us not forget who made the mold. Memory is so unreliable.

Ritter was the archetypal female sidekick: the woman's Walter Brennan, the urban Gabby Hayes, the working-class Eve Arden. Whether they called her Birdie, Stella, Mo, or Alma, her basic personality remained unchanged. We knew her type and we had a name for it: Thelma Ritter. She was the perfect partner—except for the separation anxiety she caused. Why couldn't Hollywood let her stay put? So, she wasn't a glamour-puss. Her voice, a nasal, Brooklyn-born rasp made for the delivery of the acerbic barb, has been an inspiration. It told me I didn't have to be beautiful to get attention; I just had to know when to leave a room.

Thelma knew. Okay, so her exits were scripted—that's beside the point. The thirty movies that were lucky enough to have her didn't dare let her stick around for more than a few scenes—she stole every one of them. She left a scene with grace and no complaints, even if she didn't say good-bye. Yet she remained the quintessential trouper, proof that character parts are essentially temp jobs, written out of a movie early on.

In *The Birdman of Alcatraz*, Ritter disappears from view about halfway through, when her only son, convicted killer Burt Lancaster, defies her to marry a woman Ritter dis-approves of. Up until this point, she's been his rock and redeemer. She's had the gumption to go straight to the White House to plead for a commutation of his sentence, she's traded her home in Alaska (Alaska?) for a little house down the lane from Leavenworth.

Then, just as we've come to expect, or rather hope, for her appearances between Burt's bird-infested jail scenes, enter the Other Woman. Ritter delivers the ultimate movie ultimatum—"Give her up, Robbie, forget her"—and is instantly booted from the film. We never hear another thing about her.

I looked at this movie again recently, expecting to see Ritter in her usual sardonically nurturing role, handing out shovel-fuls of tough love. Wasn't I surprised to find lovable Thelma Ritter playing a steely monster—the definitive mother from hell, the original woman who loves too much—anything but charming. In *Birdman,* her voice is quiet, clipped, and cold, oozing a barely contained slick of venomous oil. She's hate-ful—no wonder Lancaster committed murder. He probably just meant to kill his mother.

Still, Ritter is the most interesting character in the film and I couldn't help but wonder where she went. Did she stay in the little house down the lane, living out her days frustrated and bitter? Did she throw off her sad-sack dress and go on to take her revenge? We know what happens to Burt; whatever becomes of Thelma?

In the party scene of *All About Eve* that made "Fasten your seat belts—we're in for a bumpy night" so famous, she disap-pears down the stairs with a guest's fur coat over her arm (Rit-ter calls it "a dead animal act") and never comes back. Was she fired? (Not likely.) Is she ill? (Not Thelma!) Where did she go? We never know.

In *The Misfits,* she plays divorcée Marilyn Monroe's forcibly cheerful Reno landlady with both aching desperation and enormous good humor, but quickly exits the scene after she spots her character's ex-husband at a rodeo and just *has* to go meet the new wife. The movie plods on without her. It's awful.

In *Miracle on 34th Street,* her debut film, she has a cameo early on with which she establishes a precedent elemental to the story, and disappears—gone but not forgotten.

With this tiny part, as a cranky but impressionable mother

of a young boy visiting Macy's Santa Claus, Ritter managed to establish her most enduring persona. There is the funny hat and the dowdy coat she always wore; there is the unmistakable voice, the sardonic twist to the mouth, the plucky attitude and unfailing generosity that mark her characters again and again. That must be why they let her stay in *Rear Window* till the very last scene, inhabiting one of her typical background roles as Jimmy Stewart's private nurse. Our eyes ought to be riveted on the beauty of the foreground, Grace Kelly; what are we doing watching Thelma? Because she's the only one in the room who can still be surprised. Ritter is there to keep us honest. It's a shame to see her go.

In *Pillow Talk,* where she plays Doris Day's *fahblunget* dipsomaniac housekeeper, she has a big scene with Rock Hudson, during which she drinks him under the table. Remarkably, it comes near the picture's denouement. Of course, by this time she too was getting top billing. When we last see her, she's swooning before an elevator operator who just wants to go home and take care of her. Like we do.

But Ritter did not have many opportunities to enjoy happy endings. In Samuel Fuller's *Pickup on South Street,* she's killed off well before the movie's final curtain.

This awkward, if endearing, 1953 espionage-noir has Ritter traversing Cold War country as a sassy New York bag lady who sells ties on the street and trades information on the side. She's a stoolie, in other words, not usually a greatly admired profession. But every principal character in this film respects her, takes her as a confidante, protector, pal. All but one, that is—her killer.

Ritter's dying moments in *Pickup* have to be among the most affecting in the history of film. We don't actually see her take a bullet; instead, we're made to study the mortal exhaustion of a life on the street, forced to watch it creep into her dried flower of a face and make it weep.

I know I did, partly because the performance is profound and partly because I too know that kind of helpless surrender; it's what I got from an addiction to drugs, relief from which seemed to appear only in the face of death. I was lucky enough to find another escape, but *Pickup*'s Ritter meets her darker fate more nobly than I ever could. In her final moments, she gives up on herself but refuses to give in to pressure, never again to divulge her sources for any amount of money. She dies with her lips zipped. Proud Thelma.

Why should a movie want to get rid of the only character that makes it credible? Was she too Jewish? Too smart? Too clannish and rough around the edges? I know: she was too real.

She was a pistol in a hip-slung holster—pure sassafras, and her aim was true. Her snappy observations sounded funny even when she wasn't joking, though she never really was. That's what made Ritter so easy to love: her total lack of guile. I can't think of a single inauthentic moment in her whole career. Her quick barbs and early exits are pretty close to the ill-timed interruptions and pleasant surprises of life itself. Maybe too close for comfort? Not for me. I say bring her back. She was regular folks—frumpy but cute, tough as nails, and sweet as double-crusted berry pie—we need her. If life is short, it can still be good and it doesn't hurt to have a reminder.

I seldom went to movies when I was a child, as the one theater in our area was not close by. On lazy or rainy Saturday afternoons I sat in front of the television watching movies from the thirties and forties—wartime pictures and westerns, African jungle adventures, and the occasional screwball comedy. I also read every book I could get my hands on, Nancy Drews and Superman comics, Mark Twain, whatever was lying around the house: *The Diary of Anne Frank,* the collected works of Balzac, Alexander King's memoirs, a James Michener novel (he lived in the area), James Joyce.

Around the time I reached puberty, I joined a science-fiction book club. This was right after I'd seen *Invasion of the Body Snatchers* on TV. The movie had scared me silly, but the books that arrived each month tended to put less emphasis on horror than on extramarital sex, or some kind of sex, fairly graphic descriptions of which opened the only brave new world I could hope to find.

Several of these books featured future societies (and future sex), complete with aliens and all kinds of progressive gadgetry; the others imagined either a fully utopian society in which something hideous occurs to send its people hurtling dangerously toward Doom, or a world saved from self-destruction by a utopian solution that seemed to me entirely plausible and even necessary, these being the days of H-bomb tests and fallout shelters and general nuclear paranoia. Science fiction seemed the true visionary genre.

Yet I remember only one story from these books, or rather the essence of it. I don't know what it was called or who wrote it but it involved a nation, or a planet, or a town of people who all, by government fiat, had exactly the same face. Anyone exhibiting alternative characteristics, such as an interesting nose or the wrong color eyes or curly hair, was considered either a criminal or a throwback—in any case, a bad risk. One of these revolutionaries, along with his forbidden love interest (with whom he had continual and steamy sex), were the heroes of the tale. Naturally, they got into a peck of trouble, but the cause of individualism won out, and the world went on as it does, about equally divided between assholes and saints.

Thelma Ritter made a great adjudicator of these factions. We see a lot of bodies on-screen today, but not so many remarkable faces. When one comes along who looks a little different from the rest, we regard him or her as either "funny-looking" and unworthy of serious consideration, or "wholly unique" and destined for stardom. If Ritter offered no discernible sexual buzz, at least she had a face. Not a glamour-puss, just a puss. It said, "Who do you think you're kidding?"

Not Thelma.

She never displayed a sense of her own self-importance, but ego is not a job requirement for a character actor; integrity is. Ritter's was formidable, even forbidding. She never let anyone get away with anything. I study her performances for tips. I've been around the block a few times, often against my will, and there's nothing more exhilarating than being able to laugh about it. I can count on Thelma for help with that. If many of her movies were dumbfounding fluff, she was the ground for us airheads to walk on, to anchor off, to fly from. This is ground I would like to kiss, if only it weren't so fleeting.

ROGUES' GALLERY

Luc Sante

Nick Adams died young, of "an overdose of drugs he was taking for a nervous disorder," and this was entirely in character, could have been more appropriate only if he had literally exploded. In the 1950s Adams was maybe the closest thing Hollywood had to an actual beatnik, not a flaming star like James Dean, possibly a bit like an untamed Bobby Darin, much more like a guy sitting for hours in Nedick's with his leg shaking uncontrollably, ablaze with indignation at iniquities, as old as the world, that he had only lately discovered abroad in the streets. A face in the crowd in *Rebel Without a Cause* (1955), he is not remembered for any particular role (at least in films; on television he was the Civil War malcontent Johnny Yuma), except perhaps his attempting to communicate with the population of Japan in modified jive in *Frankenstein Conquers the World* (1966).

George Arliss was Richelieu, Voltaire, Disraeli, Alexander Hamilton, the Duke of Wellington. Of them all he looked most like Disraeli, but his was the generic face of history, a long face carved by wind and rain, of a sort familiar from oil portraits and now lost to central heating, refined sugars—and, of course, ideas of masculine appearance spread by the movies. He spent his film career as an apparition from the era before photography; he could command and dignify the stiffest, dullest pictures by doing nothing at all. That this was so even in the silent era is a useful measure of distance.

Wallace Beery was the canny rube, the lovable roughneck, the ugly guy who gets the girl. He was in every way a man of his time, the generation that came of age before the First World War, who still had one foot on the sodbuster's claim even as the other entered the skyscraper lobby. His kind broke chairs over each other's heads in pre–Volstead Act saloons, died at Vera Cruz and on the Marne, ran Florida real estate swindles during the Harding and Coolidge administrations, populated hobo jungles before the CCC trucked them off to make riprap. He was in hundreds of movies, from *Speedie the Swatter* (1914) to *Big Jack* (1949), and on the basis of a dozen you can figure he was consistent in all of them. His rubber-faced grin made itself at home in the most unlikely settings—*Grand Hotel*, for instance. As a duo with his female counterpart, Marie Dressler, the two of them seemed to cover the whole range of human reflexes, the low just edging out the high.

Ralph Bellamy was the other guy, the extra man, the high school pal you forgot all about until you saw his obituary, and then missed without quite knowing why. He is best remembered for the Cary Grant crack in *His Girl Friday* (1940): "What does he look like?" "He looks like Ralph Bellamy." The joke would not have worked with any other actor. Only Bellamy could fade from sight while you looked straight at him.

His was not the spy's invisibility, though, but the self-effacement of the man who left his ego in his other pair of pants. In most of his more memorable vehicles his job was to not get the girl, making him in essence a shill. He could bet any amount of the house's money so long as he lost.

William Bendix, the son of a conductor of the Metropolitan Opera orchestra, appeared as the American working class, which at the time was believed to inhabit Brooklyn. His head was approximately the size of the Rock of Gibraltar, and the heavy body underneath proportionately seemed like the bottom bit of a framed caricature at Sardi's. He could make the utterance of a four-word sentence as ponderous as the clashing of tectonic plates. Such was his archetype that I always misremembered him as playing Lenny in *Of Mice and Men*. During the war (*Guadalcanal Diary*, 1942) he was brave and he cried; after it (*The Blue Dahlia*, 1946) he was damaged, an unwitting tool deployed by bad men. Later (*The Life of Riley*, 1949), he, along with his constituency, repaired to bus driving and television and leisure.

Eddie Bracken was always preceded by his ears and his Adam's apple; not far behind were his crooked grin, his orbiting eyes, and whatever chaos-theory disposition passed for his coiffure on any given day. He stood somewhere between a Boy Scout and Alfred E. Neuman, an All-American simpleton ready to take the rap and to pose proudly for pictures while doing so. He wasn't a patsy, exactly; maybe he just spoke for the patsy in every voter's heart. His career barely outlasted the 1940s. Preston Sturges made the best use of him (*The Miracle of Morgan's Creek* and *Hail the Conquering Hero,* both 1944).

The national *amour-propre* might not have withstood the denting he would have given it as an adult figure.

Neville Brand was an exceedingly convincing sociopath. He had many teeth, and displayed them to advantage. He exuded intelligence, and you knew he would have broken all of your fingers one by one, slowly and while chuckling. His finest role was in Don Siegel's *Riot in Cell Block 11* (1954; commemorated in the Lieber-Stoller song, renumbered for scansion), which allowed him to balance sinner and sinned-against with a complexity not allowed for even by counter-type. You got a whole history with this guy. You saw the unelectrified farmhouse where his uncle beat him with a razor strop, the juvenile institution where he was tied to the bed for his neighbor's torts, the alley where his confederates turned rat and left him to die—none of which is borne out by his biography.

El Brendel was a vaudeville comedian who often relied on a yumpin'-yiminy Scandinavian shtick that was fading when he was in diapers a century ago, so that he was too late to ride Weber and Fields's capacious coattails to success on the boards. In Raoul Walsh's *The Big Trail* (1930), a movie in which historical authenticity is—brilliantly—metonymized by theatrical bombast, he appears alongside the legendary Tyrone Power, Sr., among other revenants from the Bowery stages of the 1870s, in contrast to the underplaying new men led by the young John Wayne. He wasn't merely a human artifact, though; he had about him something of the Shakespearean clown, but he always seemed misplaced in time. He acted as late as 1956, in *The She Creature*, of all things.

Raymond Burr was more than Perry Mason and Ironside—

or rather he played the same role in films for a decade beforehand. He was usually a villain then (you remember him in *Rear Window*), although that made little difference. He was always the sunken-eyed mask, the rumbling baritone, the massive body that pounded along like a golem. His bulk made him a continent unto himself, in the vastness of whose steppes such refinements as good and evil simply dissolved. You got the feeling that, in life, wherever you stood in relation to him he would always be facing you, the three-dimensional equivalent of one of those paintings whose eyes follow you around the room. He would have made a better Goldfinger, a plausible Dr. Moreau, an excellent Dr. Mabuse.

John Carradine, it is said, walked the streets of Hollywood, rapidly scissoring his endless drainpipe legs, loudly declaiming Shakespeare. This was fully in character; he became his own type, although he was really a much better actor than the type would suggest. But that figure—the overweening ham, a Lincolnesque skeleton in black, tormented by the succubi of his art—could be inserted anywhere, and it was, from *Tol'able David* (1930) to *The Tomb* (1986), from *The Sign of the Cross* (1932) to *Vampire Hookers* (1978), from *The Garden of Allah* (1936) to *The Astro-Zombies* (1968). His impeccable diction and fanatical stare could always be counted on to frighten the yokels and tickle the philistines. A living artifact of the era of D. W. Griffith planted in the midst of frantically gyrating teenagers, he could stand as a one-man *Sunset Boulevard*. After all, by the 1950s Hollywood's most potent image of horror was its own past.

Leo G. Carroll wore his middle initial the way he wore his

homburg, as a badge of respectability improbably converted into panache. Hitchcock, who went in for definitive characterizations, used him in six pictures, from *Rebecca* (1940) to *North by Northwest* (1959), usually as a sort of apotheosis of the civil servant. Carroll conveyed an authority that verged on omniscience, a restraint that contained worlds. He could speak while moving only the very middle of his lower lip. If you believe in heaven you can imagine him manning the admissions desk.

Jack Carson was a big guy with a breezy manner that did little to obscure an overwhelming impression of guilt. His roles usually called for him to be in the way, as a tinhorn, a used-car salesman, an eavesdropping neighbor, an untrustworthy confidant, a coward, an opportunist, a sponger, a leech. He was frequently to be seen justifying his actions, smoothing over troublesome facts, blithely hail-fellow in moments of crisis, attempting to unload a bill of goods. Frighteningly authentic in his embodiment of the worst American traits, he appeared in numerous westerns, comedies, musicals, films noir; see for example *Mildred Pierce* (1945).

Richard Conte was the tuna with good taste. His minions were always waking him up in the middle of the night, and he would appear in the marble entrance hall in his satin dressing gown, not a hair out of place, to reproach them in low tones, fastidiously polite. He could convey more threat with good manners than any hundred thugs could manage with a razor and a gat. You could figure his characters to have somehow leaped from messenger-boy stickups to fine-wine connoisseurship in a single bound. The decor was strictly from Vegas: lots of bogus Louis Quinze and ormolu candlesticks and bas-relief putti. Sometimes the act was regulation wise-guy and sometimes, as in Joseph H. Lewis's *The Big Combo* (1955), it suggested unimaginable baroque depths of evil.

Andy Devine appeared in several thousand westerns as a good-hearted dope. His biggest asset was his voice, a high-pitched rasp that sounded like an unoiled power tool and was apparently the result of a childhood accident. It was a kindly rasp nevertheless, with a hesitant quality that could make him appear feeble-minded, and Devine always wore his body like an outsized suit of clothes, so that he could be mistaken for an anthropomorphized bear or a permanent toddler. He was employed numerous times by John Ford, sidekicked for Guy Madison and Roy Rogers, hosted a kids' TV variety show set in a barn. Babies everywhere trusted him implicitly.

Jean Hersholt started out as a stage actor in Denmark and appeared in films for forty years, but he is chained in memory to a single role, that of Dr. Paul Christian, the kindly country general practitioner. White-haired and deliberate, with a benign twinkle and a soft accent, he rose to the sound of knocking at midnight, traversed long distances on back roads, laid his hand on feverish brows, drew sheets up over recumbent forms. The very idea of this character seems as remote today as the pince-nez and the bustle, and the films are seldom shown. But Hersholt apparently had something in common with his character. He was given to good works. After his death the Academy of Motion Picture Arts and Sciences established the Jean Hersholt Humanitarian Award, a tool it deploys much the way the Vatican uses the plenary indulgence.

Burl Ives sang "Tumbling Tumbleweeds" and "The Blue-Tail Fly." He sported a goatee and a plaid shirt, strange bohemian affectations in the darkness of postwar America, but nobody gave him any guff about it because he was the size of three men. As a folk singer he was your uncle, basically, but when he broke into films he did not take long to establish himself as a singularly frightening and overwhelming villain. His banner year was 1958, when he appeared in both *Wind Across the Everglades* and *Cat on a Hot Tin Roof.* He was a force of nature. His Big Daddy in the latter picture might have sired every axe murderer south of the Mason-Dixon Line.

Tully Marshall was born during the Civil War and died during World War II. He was a gnarled stick-insect Yankee who was cast as bishops, bumpkins, drug addicts, aristocrats, and madmen, such was his range and such was the impression he gave of totemically embodying a whole world outside the audience's ken. Erich von Stroheim best sounded the sinister abyss he suggested, casting him, for example, in *Queen Kelly* as the most corrupt specimen of European degradation in a rancid colony in East Africa, a man—pierced and tattooed, as it happens—who is never seen without a whip in one hand and a whiskey bottle in the other. Underlying his menace was the fact that he looked like a product of intensive breeding, that caprice shared by troglodytes and royalty.

Victor Mature was a big, handsome Italian boy from Brooklyn—actually he was from Louisville and of Swiss extraction, but you know what I mean. He came along as a studly archetype in the postwar years when white ethnicity was becoming acceptable, and his curly hair, flaring nostrils, and excellent teeth were instruments of a wholesome sort of predigested exotica. He never appeared very intelligent, and whether or not this was the case in life it was a distinct asset in his film career. It meant, for one thing, that he could effortlessly traffic between eras in costume pictures—per Hollywood, the past's population was composed of one part sages to fifty parts brutes. So he was the superior, well-meaning brute: e.g., Samson, a credit to his class.

Edmond O'Brien played more or less the same role for about thirty-five years, a role assigned him by his physiognomy. He was the irate, hoarse, sweaty, rumpled urban semiprofessional in crime pictures, westerns, and even *Julius Caesar* (as Casca; 1953). He, too, was superior to his type—but on the other hand you can imagine him as a bassoon. The bassoon is a very particular instrument; you would not prefer that it be a flute. O'Brien brought an abrasive texture, one often much needed, into every movie. He conveyed a certain trustworthiness of character, even when cast as cowards or drunks, of a core honesty even when lying. His one memorable lead came in *D.O.A.* (1950), playing a man who has been poisoned and has only twenty-four hours to find the perpetrator and thus the antidote, a ludicrous proposition he managed to make credible.

Michael J. Pollard devised and incarnated a type that arguably had not officially existed before he came on-screen. He looked like a gnome, was frequently larcenous and usually stoned, suggested all manner of mundane flatland corruption and pure-products-of-America-go-crazy. He started showing up in movies in the early '60s, appearing most memorably in

The Wild Angels (1966) and *Bonnie and Clyde* (1967). After that you saw Pollard figures everywhere. He sold you crushed aspirin in front of the Fillmore; he bummed everybody out at the collective tripping party in the woods; there might have been two or three of him on the fringes of the Manson family. He did not simply deal in bad vibes, of course—he could equally well hand you a laugh. You would nevertheless look for the barb in it. Although he has continued to act, he is doomed to remain in some fashion a human time capsule for the year 1969.

George Sanders is now possibly better known for having killed himself on account of boredom than for any of his films, but the beauty of it is that the gesture itself comes straight out of his cinematic repertory. He made about a zillion pictures, many of them awful. In them he stood for culture and refinement and worldliness in ways that fulfilled the contempt of the average consumer of popcorn. All over the wilds of America he hung as an effigy labeled "Europe." He seemed to have been born jaded, to have been to the opera more times than he had been to the bathroom. He played Landru, Bel-Ami, numerous Nazis; his second wife was Zsa Zsa Gabor (and his fourth was her sister Magda); his autobiography was called *Memoirs of a Professional Cad*. You could not imagine him in more than a handful of physical postures—any garment other than a dinner jacket made him look naked. Until very recently there were still drama critics who modeled their personae after his character in *All About Eve* (1950).

Akim Tamiroff may not have invented the pan-ethnic character type, but until he passed the baton to Anthony Quinn in the 1950s he owned the franchise. Born in Azerbaijan and trained in the Moscow Art Theater, he came to America in the 1920s and very soon found himself playing improbable Chinese figures in Hollywood. His genius was for comedy, and this underlay his acting even in pictures of such dead seriousness as *For Whom the Bell Tolls* (1943), in which his villainous Pablo (he always seemed to be playing men named Pablo) becomes affecting by being cut just short of buffoonishness. He had a great way with cartoon explosions of sputtering rage—his exclamation of "Samson and Delilah—Sodom and Gomorrah!" in Preston Sturges's *The Great McGinty* (1940) is one of the indelible sound bites of cinematic history. Every immigrant should study his films to appreciate just how to use a foreign accent to advantage.

Lee Van Cleef, of Somerville, New Jersey, was one of those actors who unjustly languished in small parts at home but found true stature on the Italian frontier in the untamed 1960s, beginning with the iconic Sergio Leone cycle. He was excellent at narrowing his eyes; he narrowed his eyes definitively. He narrowed them because it indicated villainy, because the desert wind was blowing his way, because he wanted to shoot someone standing a great distance off in the sun, because he could awaken in spectators some atavistic fear going back to Genghis Khan. He made crime pictures and westerns, period. Nobody ever tried to shoehorn him into a romantic comedy or a teenage beach romp or even a monster movie. Nobody would have dared; it would have been like flavoring the cake with slivovitz.

Keenan Wynn always stepped into a picture like a thirty-year professional taking over a crime scene from the rookies. That is, he seldom gave the appearance of acting, but bustled about and barked orders as if he were intruding on some pantomimed nonsense in order to fix a vital problem. He made an impression on audiences not as an artist but as an authority figure, which in itself is proof of his high artistry. Such was his anti-star virtuoso competence that it is difficult to pick out any particular role from a forty-year career that spanned most of the available genres. He looked a bit like John Steinbeck—mustache, cowlick, neck—and often worked territory not too far from the novelist's, but unlike Steinbeck he was never hamstrung by sentimentality.

ELMER FUDD

David Hajdu

I get a feeling when I watch one of the old Warner Bros. cartoons, and the closest I can come to describing it is a Russian
word, *razlyubit*. It refers to a certain affection one always
retains for the first person one loved. Growing up in the three-
channel suburbia of northwestern New Jersey during the early
1960s, when local affiliates used syndicated cartoon packages
to fill the time between toy and candy-bar commercials in the
after-school hours, I learned most of what I first knew about
film comedy from the nearly one thousand animated shorts
produced under the Looney Tunes and Merrie Melodies trade-
marks between 1930 and 1964. Warner closed up the bunga-
low clubhouse where directors such as Friz Freleng, Chuck
Jones, and Robert McKimson long conspired to create Bugs
Bunny, Daffy Duck, Porky Pig, and the Road Runner, abandoning production in favor of marketing and distribution, as
all the studios had already done for feature films. In the same
year Lyndon Johnson was elected president, the Beatles took
over the record charts, Cassius Clay defeated Sonny Liston for
the World Heavyweight Championship, and my sister got her
first boyfriend. It was a period of tumult for us all, one way or

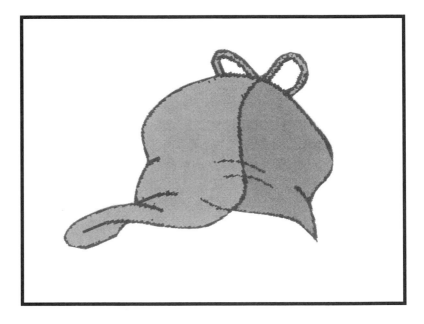

another; fortunately, the vintage Warner Bros. cartoons, fixed in the timeless other of cartoon Hollywood, provided certain respite every day before dinner. In six and a half minutes, each of the shorts—or the better among them, since all aren't equally inspired—knowingly exploited and parodied the studio system that had, for decades, been the entertainment universe. Looney Tunes developed its own stars, the biggest being Bugs, the cavalier Brooklyn rabbit, and Daffy, the manically vainglorious duck, whose casual interaction with caricatures of real-life screen actors such as Humphrey Bogart and Edward G. Robinson served to reinforce the cartoon characters' stature and illuminate the actors' cartoonishness. (One of Bugs's animated friends sees him on a park bench next to Bing Crosby, Eddie Cantor, Jack Benny, and Al Jolson, and he says, "Bugs Bunny—why are you hanging around with these guys? They'll never amount to anything.") In ostensible behind-the-scenes stories, Looney Tunes characters would squabble over studio business with a brazen virulence unseen in contemporary newsreels of flesh-and-blood Hollywood families smiling by the pool. (Threatening to leave Warner's, Porky Pig asks his boss, "What's Errol Flynn got that I haven't?" That both spent most of their time without pants goes unspoken.) Of course, Warner's cartoon studio also included a regular supporting player: a strange, lonely animated human in a realm of anthropomorphic celebrity, Elmer Fudd.

After a few years of awkward experimentation as a profoundly silly figure alternately called both Elmer Fudd and Egghead, he took full form in a 1940 Bugs Bunny short, "A

Wild Hare"; from then on, he appeared as permutations of the same character in a fairly wide range of story situations. While the Looney Tunes stars (Bugs, Daffy, Porky Pig, Sylvester, and company) were usually featured as themselves, Elmer costarred as a hunter, a Mountie, a scientist, a hotel manager, or a farmer. In "The Hardship of Miles Standish" (1940), a knockabout twist on Longfellow's nineteenth-century poem, he portrayed pilgrim John Alden; in "What's Opera, Doc?" (1957), Chuck Jones's scathing parody of Wagner's *Der Ring des Nibelungen*, he sang ("Kill the wabbit!") as the warrior Siegfried. Elmer Fudd became the character actor among actor characters. Whatever his role, however, Elmer—like Mickey Rooney in Warner's stock-company version of *A Midsummer Night's Dream* or John Wayne in George Stevens's biblical epic, *The Greatest Story Ever Told*—retained his elemental Fuddness.

A grown man old enough to have gone completely bald, Elmer J. Fudd is an oversized newborn, proportionally and psychologically. His head is a fruit bowl of round shapes: honeydew cheeks, plum nose, cantaloupe eyes on a blue-ribbon Crenshaw head. In a live-action film, Elmer would be Guy Kibbee (the governor in *Mr. Smith Goes to Washington*) or Henry Travers (the angel Clarence in *It's a Wonderful Life*). His wide-open, blinking eyes signal the work of a slow mind, although Fudd is not cartoon-dumb in that goofy (or Goofy) "Which way did he go?" way; Elmer is an innocent, not an idiot. The only adult human in the Warner cartoon world, he is the most like a child. (Fudd's speech impediment, wherein *r*'s and sometimes *l*'s are spoken as *w*'s—"You scwewy wabbit!"—

occurs commonly among preschoolers.) However, Elmer's infantility does not seem designed to help children to relate to him. As directors Freleng and Jones frequently explained, their animated shorts were not made for kids, nor for adults, but for themselves. Moreover, in his supporting capacity, one of Elmer's principal functions is to enlarge the hero (say, Bugs) through self-reduction. He may be cast as a titular figure of authority or hold a kind of power (say, a shotgun) at the onset of the film—the boss to the adults in the audience, the grown-up to kids—but he will inevitably lose out in the end, largely by virtue of his own inability. During the Second World War, Warner director Bob Clampett attributed a boom in the popularity of Bugs Bunny cartoons to audiences' association of the scrappy, ever-triumphant prey, Bugs, with American GIs and the hapless predator, Elmer, with the Axis powers; Elmer, Chuck Jones added, even looked something like Mussolini.

In American film, the great sentimentalists—Chaplin, Disney, Capra, and Spielberg (as well as their innumerable imitators, particularly Jerry Lewis and John Hughes)—have glamorized a romantic conception of childhood as a more innocent, that is, purer, therefore, higher state of being than adulthood; in their work, age corrupts and most of what we associate with maturity (sex, career, culture) is rendered suspect. At Looney Tunes, a contrary view predominates: Elmer, the studio's prominent symbol of childlike innocence, suffers mightily for his immaturity. (Tweety Bird, though very young, is smarter than his grown adversary, Sylvester the Cat.) By nature open-minded, trusting, sensitive, and forgiving, Elmer is congenitally ill-equipped to compete with Bugs, the image of savvy, charm, quick wit, and resourcefulness, not to mention duplicity. In Disney's hands, Elmer's puerility, like the essential simple-mindedness of Mickey Mouse, Donald Duck, Goofy, Pluto—in other words, almost all Disney characters except for the villains, most of whom are awfully dumb, too—would, before the end credits, prove to be his redemption; at Warner's, it's his undoing. I remember hearing my big brother call Elmer a "dummy" and a "loser" when I was a kid, and I'm glad he made that association between the two traits; it's one my own two children haven't gotten much from television in the 1990s.

An exceptional character in-house at Warner, as well, Elmer Fudd was not voiced by actor Mel Blanc, who handled the characterizations for almost all other males in the Looney Tunes stable and who was generally the only vocal performer acknowledged in the Warner cartoon credits. Working anonymously, comic character actor Arthur Q. Bryan devised the sad, dysphasic voice that evokes Elmer instantly and has been inextricably associated with him for six decades—a low-energy baritone mix of croak and tremor, with wots of wowds pwonounced wike that. Bryan, who looked even more like Elmer Fudd than Mussolini, used several voices in convincing portrayals of various sorts of dullards in countless radio shows, a handful of films (nearly all forgotten programmers such as 1940's *Millionaire Playboy* and 1944's *I'm from Arkansas*), and a few episodes of TV series, most notably an *I Love Lucy* in which he makes a rare appearance using Elmer's voice as a different character. Shortly before Bryan's death at sixty in 1959, Warner's began trying out others as Elmer, including Mel

Blanc (who had filled in for Bryan on a few occasions), though none brought the character quite the same helpless élan.

Chuck Jones, one of more than a dozen Looney Tunes and Merrie Melodies directors who used Elmer to varying degrees, is responsible for nearly all of his most memorable appearances: those in "The Scarlet Pumpernickel" (1950), "The Rabbit of Seville" (1950), "Beanstalk Bunny" (1955), "What's Opera, Doc?" "Bugs Bonnets" (1956), and the trilogy of Daffy-Bugs hunting-season confrontations, "Rabbit Fire" (1951), "Rabbit Seasoning" (1952), and "Duck! Rabbit! Duck!" (1953). While Jones has written extensively about his life and work in two memoirs, *Chuck Amuck* (1989) and *Chuck Reducks* (1996), he scarcely mentions Elmer. "Daffy Duck is a rueful recognition of my own (and your own) ineptitudes. Bugs Bunny is a glorious personification of our most dapper dreams," Jones theorized. "We love Daffy because he is us, we love Bugs because he is as wonderful as we would like to be." What about Elmer Fudd? Neither our cartoon self-reflection nor our dream image, he is not us at all, by design; an anti-Everyman, he's the Other Guy through whom we identify ourselves only by rejection.

In the 1950s, Looney Tunes' creative use of Elmer as a negative force, a character through whom given ideas could be discredited by ridicule, approached cultural insurgency. At a time when popular entertainment reinforced the postwar ideal of cozy suburban prosperity with TV series such as *The Adventures of Ozzie and Harriet* and *Father Knows Best,* none of the Warner cartoon characters followed that American Dream, except Elmer Fudd. His goals were the middle-class aspirations of the Eisenhower era: he tried to keep a nice house, do his job ("Oh deaw!" he cries in 1954's "Design for Leaving," "I'w be wate for wowk!"), and unwind on the weekends; even his hunting was recast as an idle pastime ("I'm a vegetawian— I onwy hunt fow spowt"). His antagonists, Bugs, Daffy, and Sylvester, clearly hold Elmer's conservative pursuits in contempt and zealously undermine them through street wile (Bugs), anarchy (Daffy), and connivance (Sylvester). For those of us watching at an impressionable age, the message was persuasively subversive: the only one behaving like our parents, doing everything they told us to do, was the fool.

Then there's the gay thing. Much has been made of Bugs Bunny's cross-dressing and flirting with male characters, particularly Elmer. The lead characters ponder Bugs's feminine sex appeal in the movie *Wayne's World* (1992), and animation scholar Kevin S. Sandler has written a thorough essay on the topic of Bugs's sexuality in the anthology he edited about Warner animation, *Reading the Rabbit* (1998). Bugs adopts drag thirty-six times and kisses twenty-eight male and four female figures, Sandler points out. Yet, for Bugs, sex is essentially another of his tricks; he plants a surprise kiss on a male opponent's lips (whether he is Elmer or Yosemite Sam) to disarm, confuse, or humiliate him, and he dolls up and seduces foes to gain power over them. Bugs manipulates gender and employs sex tactically, but he always returns to a clear-cut male role by the end of the cartoon.

Elmer also crosses gender barriers, but in a significantly different way. When Elmer responds amorously to a male overture or dons a woman's clothes, it is an act of submission; he is giving in to a romantic impulse, not pretending to be something he's not. Bugs and Elmer go so far as to marry in two cartoons ("The Rabbit of Seville" and "Bugs Bonnets"), Bugs the groom (retaining his male identity), Elmer an ecstatic bride. Is the animators' intent to deride homosexuality by associating it with Elmer? Probably. Then again, both of these cartoons use the image of Bugs and Elmer happily wed as their climactic, closing messages. "You know," Bugs explains with a smile, "I think it always helps a picture to have a romantic ending."

I'm surprised that there's been so little critical discourse about Elmer Fudd, what with two generations raised on TV cartoons now heading the university pop-culture (and gender) studies departments. The reference book *Looney Tunes and Merrie Melodies: A Complete Illustrated Guide to the Warner Bros. Cartoons* by Jerry Beck and Will Friedwald pictures all the popular Warner characters except Elmer on its cover and omits him from its character index. At what remains of the Warner Bros. studio, a string of new cartoons with the classic characters was produced in the 1990s, keeping the licensed merchandise franchise alive, although none features Elmer in more than token cameos. As a licensed merchandise commodity, too, he is represented on some half-dozen of the thousands of geegaws I saw for sale at the Warner Bros. Studio store on Manhattan's Fifth Avenue. "Duh," my twelve-year-old daughter said to me, pithily. "Who wants Elmer stuff? He *is* Elmer." Well, duh, indeed. Perhaps there is some recompense in the prospect that his famous costars are who they are at least partly because of him. At the very least, he seems to be getting what he always wanted: west and wewaxation at wast.

WARNER BROS.' FAT MEN

Dana Gioia

"Imprisoned in every fat man," claimed Cyril Connolly, "a thin one is wildly signaling to be let out." Connolly, himself a literary mandarin of considerable girth, made this observation half a century ago in *The Unquiet Grave* (1945), but his dictum easily summarizes Hollywood's current philosophy on weight. A fat man is a failed thin one. Hollywood has taken the Duchess of Windsor's remark that "No woman can be too rich or too thin" and made it a royal decree that applies to both sexes. Our stars have never been richer or thinner.

May one lone fan raise an objection? I don't mind the eye-popping salaries. Only a cheapskate would resent eight-figure per-film fees to artists of such magnitude as Jim Carrey or Julia Roberts. Where would Hollywood stars be without their mansions, ranches, and villas? What I miss are the full-figured actors of yesteryear. The few fat men still around seem visibly unhappy about their size. Their greatest performances occur mostly off-camera as they diet agonizingly in a vain effort to be slender. Tom Arnold does not look better thin—just older, more worn, and a little lumpy. We want our stars to radiate desire for sex, money, and adventure—not for dessert. Nowadays no one is safe. Even Godzilla had to lose his trademark beer-belly for the 1998 remake. How sad to watch movies where even the heavies are skinnies.

In the Hollywood I love best, fat men filled the Silver Screen, innocent and unabashed. Few of these oversize talents played leads, though some managed top billing, but they all knew there were no small parts, only small actors. Tinseltown was sweeter in those Great Depression days. The rich didn't go hungry, and audiences got more actor for their money. A roly-poly man wasn't clinically obese but amiable, and a jowly butterball like S. Z. Sakall could affectionately be nicknamed "Cuddles."

I like to imagine these hefty heroes gathering in the afterlife. The feasting hall of their B-budget Valhalla is the original Wilshire Boulevard Brown Derby secretly rescued by Valkyries from the wrecker's ball. As they file in (to the accompaniment of Miklos Rozsa's "Bread and Circus March" from *Ben-Hur*) for porterhouse steaks and lobsters thermidor, cherries jubilee, and baked Alaska, I mentally note their names— Edward Arnold, Monty Woolley, Charles Coburn, Sydney Greenstreet, Eugene Pallette, W. C. Fields, Oliver Hardy, Charles Laughton, Orson Welles, Wallace Beery, William Bendix, Andy Devine, Robert Morley, Edmund Gwenn, S. Z. "Cuddles" Sakall, Burl Ives, Francis L. Sullivan, Sebastian Cabot, Robert Greig, and all five of the Three Stooges. With nary a pratfall, Roscoe Arbuckle serves the hors d'oeuvres, and Alfred Hitchcock makes a momentary cameo as the waiter serving their double martinis. Some were born fat. Others achieved fatness. Some had fatness sneak up on them. But in those pre-

Cinemascope days each bestrode the narrow screen like a colossus. We shall never see their like again. The movies, as Gloria Swanson might say, have grown too small for them.

The members of this stout company now sustain reputations of varying size—from genuine fame to almost total obscurity. Welles and Hardy remain cinematic icons (as does Hollywood's most famous walk-on extra, Mr. Hitchcock). Fields, Laughton, Beery, and Arnold still enjoy eminence— roughly in that order—among the cognoscenti. There are many degrees of oblivion. Most of these actors, however, have faded in the collective memory. Although not all ships sail as swiftly Lethewards, their ultimate fate is that of Robert Greig. Film buffs may recognize the portly pompous butler, but only a few scholars or old-timers will remember his name. *Sic transit gloria Hollywoodis.*

I admire every actor at my celestial banquet. Each deserves the critical equivalent of a full-course testimonial dinner, but I want to single out two men for special attention—Sydney Greenstreet (1875–1954) and Eugene Pallette (1889–1954). To choose only one actor would seem abstemious in such hearty company. Neither actor was ever a headliner, nor have they received much attention in the now immense scholarship on American film. But both were genuine stars in the era when studios prized great character actors almost as much as matinee idols. Neither the most famous nor the most obscure men on my celestial guest list, Pallette and Greenstreet embody the qualities I most admire in character actors—personality, range, radiance, and collegiality.

Both Pallette and Greenstreet possessed a singular and

striking personality. Pallette could anchor a scene just by walking downstairs. When he enters Preston Sturges's *The Lady Eve* (1941), trotting downstairs to breakfast singing a merry ballad, he embodies all the small human hopes that screwball comedy exists to shatter. Greenstreet could be equally memorable just by leaning immensely forward in his chair. He could make the most offhand remark seem threatening or mysterious. Both actors also possessed that special radiance of the true star. In defining beauty Thomas Aquinas describes the radiant clarity that occurs when the inner identity of a thing shines forth in its true form. One never loses Greenstreet or Pallette in a crowded scene. Their personalities radiate forth. (How dimly, by comparison, most current character actors glimmer.) And yet both men were expert ensemble players. A great weakness in many character actors is that they cannot work their magic without stealing a scene. It is impossible to watch the complex ensemble scenes with Greenstreet in *The Maltese Falcon*—where he completes a virtuoso quartet with Humphrey Bogart, Peter Lorre, and Mary Astor—without admiring his collegial flexibility. And what a pleasure to follow Pallette through half a dozen complex scenes in *Mr. Smith Goes to Washington* (1939) alongside his gifted colleagues Edward Arnold, Claude Rains, William Demarest, and Guy Kibbee: he asserts himself brilliantly without ever upstaging his partners. Finally, these two actors had range. They could play fundamentally different roles without losing their quintessential individuality. The fate of most character actors is to play one particular role consummately—forever. (Consider the irresistible Franklin Pangborn flustered and flummoxed endlessly.) Pallette and Greenstreet, however, were fully developed actors equally adept at portraying scoundrels, clergymen, criminals, politicians, policemen, soldiers, and tycoons.

Although Greenstreet made considerably fewer films than Pallette, he looms larger today because he appeared in two of the most enduringly popular films Warner Bros. ever produced, *The Maltese Falcon* (1941) and *Casablanca* (1942). Greenstreet had the good fortune to make his screen debut under the guidance of another debutant, director John Huston. For his first feature, Huston had assembled a talented, quirky, and inexpensive cast to perform his screenplay of Dashiell Hammett's detective novel (which had already been filmed twice with no significant commercial success). Greenstreet was sixty-one, a veteran of the stage. Weighing in at 357 pounds, he caused consternation in the wardrobe department, and the head office worried that his inexperience would slow production. The studio never expected the B-budget remake to be a major success. Its box-office power launched Greenstreet's late-starting cinematic career. His performance as the urbane but insidious Kaspar Gutman was notably popular among both audiences and reviewers. (Note both puns in the name of Sam Spade's hefty nemesis.) At once mysterious, menacing, and amusing, his criminal adventurer still ranks as one of film's classic villains. His performance earned him his first and only Academy Award nomination.

Greenstreet lost his Oscar to Donald Crisp for *How Green Was My Valley,* but *The Maltese Falcon* earned him a considerable raise from the notoriously tight-fisted Jack Warner. Over the next ten years he went on to play a series of sophisticated villains, eloquent mystery men, and jovial bigwigs for Warner's. In *Casablanca* he played Ferrari, the local underworld chief, who owned The Blue Parrot. ("Cuddles" Sakall, by the way, worked as headwaiter for the competition, Rick's Café Américain.) Anyone who doubts Greenstreet's power should listen carefully to the generic bad-guy lines he had to deliver when the Laszlos ask his aid in escaping Morocco. Greenstreet makes every second-hand phrase sound not merely credible but evocative. In *They Died With Their Boots On* (1941) he plays General Winfield Scott opposite Errol Flynn's George Custer. (They "meet cute" sharing a dish of creamed Bermuda onions.) He begins the role exuberantly but ends with understated pathos. Perhaps his oddest role was "the Inspector" in the allegorical film *Between Two Worlds* (1944), in which dead souls sail in a spooky luxury liner toward the next world. Today this film is remembered mostly for two things—Greenstreet's harrowing performance and Erich Wolfgang Korngold's sumptuously romantic music (the composer's favorite among his eighteen Warner Bros.' scores). The young Rod Serling must have remembered *Between Two Worlds*, however, since Greenstreet's persona is recapitulated in several *Twilight Zone* episodes, though never so memorably as in the original.

No actor ever carried his fat more magisterially than Greenstreet. Erect, urbane, and self-possessed, he presents corpulence not as a liability but as an accomplishment. He is not obese but Olympian. The best interpretive artists are not always the most lavishly gifted. Fred Astaire could sing only an octave, and Billie Holiday had trouble keeping pitch. But the great interpreters understand that since their imperfections cannot be hidden, they must be used for expressive effect. When Lionel Barrymore became crippled by injury and arthritis, he turned his wheelchair-bound body into the powerful symbol of repressed anger, chronic pain, and frustrated ambition that animates his enduring performances in *It's a Wonderful Life* (1946) and *Key Largo* (1948). By contrast, Marlon Brando wears his extra weight as an annoying encumbrance. His corpulence annoys us precisely because it remains *extra*, never fully assimilated into the performer's identity. Greenstreet never tried to act around his weight. He made it so intrinsic to his identity that it seemed not only stylish but handsome. Beauty, he understood, is the truth finding expression in its perfect form. Greenstreet's rich bass voice and perfect diction also drew its distinction from his enormous physique. No small man could have ever spoken with such supernal authority.

In our calorie-conscious age, the language of corpulence has become impoverished. We make do with a few mostly clinical terms—*obese, overweight, heavy, chubby*. If the adjectival form of *fat* has not yet reached the status of obscene, it has already crossed over into the grossly impolite. Once there must have been a word adequate to describe Eugene Pallette's amazing physique, but it will not be found in current low-fat American. *Portly* seems insufficient and *tubby* too tame. Pallette came as close to globular as a human being can and still walk upright. Yet there was nothing flabby about his conspicuous girth. Round he may have been, but Pallette remained feisty and determined. After all, he had started in Hollywood as an action hero.

A trim, young Pallette enjoyed some success in silent films. He played Prosper Latour, the Huguenot cavalier, in D. W. Griffith's *Intolerance* (1916), and Aramis—to Douglas Fairbanks's D'Artagnan—in *The Three Musketeers* (1921). His best performances, however, came much later in his career. It took the now overweight actor years to settle into his mature identity. He worked for every major studio and with scores of directors in mysteries, westerns, comedies, biopics, costume dramas, and musicals. His early talkies, like the four Philo Vance mysteries he made at Warner's with William Powell, show a gifted but hardly unforgettable character actor. There are many ways of being fat, and only gradually Pallette learned that none of the conventional film types fit him very well.

Pallette eventually took the liabilities that had ruined his career as a leading man and shaped them into an unforgettable persona. His weight had been only part of the problem. By middle age Pallette had developed the voice of a human bullfrog. A matinee idol may sound pleasingly generic. (Could you imagine Rich Little doing a Harrison Ford or Robert Taylor imitation?) But a great character actor thrives on a distinctive voice. Pallette spoke half an octave below anyone else in the cast. No matter how many voices mixed in a scene, you never confuse him with another actor.

The mature Pallette character is a creature of provocative contradictions—tough-minded but indulgent, earthy but epicurean, relaxed but excitable. His grit-and-gravel voice sounds simultaneously tough and comic. Even his corpulence is two-sided. In his best films Pallette made his fatness seem like a sign of moderation and common sense. As Friar Tuck in *The*

Adventures of Robin Hood (1938) or Fray Felipe in *The Mark of Zorro* (1940), he shows that a fat priest is no heartless zealot but understands the sins of the flesh. Playing a tubby millionaire like the beer baron in *The Lady Eve* or Alexander Bullock in *My Man Godfrey* (1936), Pallette's girth gives him a common touch. Stuffed into a tuxedo that seems perpetually near bursting, he seems more down-to-earth than the stylish high society types who surround him. Even Pallette's villains, like the corrupt and cynical politico Chick McCann in *Mr. Smith Goes to Washington*, are immensely likable. Pushed too far, Pallette confidently uses his weight for physical force. When Bullock finally evicts the freeloading Carlo (Mischa Auer) in *My Man Godfrey*, we are not so much surprised as reassured by Pallette's manly strength. In battle his sword-wielding Friar Tuck is a glory to behold.

Pallette and Greenstreet both died in 1954. Each had retired a few years earlier due to age and ill health. Pallette made his last two films, *Suspense* and *In Old Sacramento*, in 1946—the first for Monogram and the second for Republic, two of the worst studios in Hollywood. Plagued by diabetes and Bright's disease, Greenstreet ended his brief cinematic career in 1949 with the marvelously awful *Flamingo Road* for Warner's and the well-cast but forgettable *Malaya* for MGM. A year earlier the Supreme Court had ordered the major motion picture companies to divest themselves of their theater chains. Television had already started to drain away the audience and change the economics of the entertainment industry. The studio era of American film was over. Fat men might find a single comic character role to repeat weekly on television, but the system that allowed Greenstreet, Pallette, and others challenging roles no longer existed. Fat men had to be funny or— except for Raymond Burr—find another career. We lost Charles Laughton and got Drew Carey. Funny is okay, but what does it say about our culture that at a time when the average American has never been heavier the only part an overweight actor can play is a clown? John Goodman is the only serious actor who has escaped this stereotyping, and for all we know he is probably on a diet.

FRANKLIN PANGBORN: AN APOLOGIA

Siri Hustvedt

I don't know when Mr. Franklin Pangborn first came to my attention. A man of the screen's margins, his legacy comes of repetitions. He pops up in one movie here, in another over there. He rules a moment or a full-fledged scene, never an entire film. It was only after I had seen many American films of the thirties and forties that his name came to signify the pompous underling for whom I have come to feel affection. I like the reliability of his character, and I like his name. It combines the elevated connotations of Franklin, as in Ben and Roosevelt, with the pathos of "pang," and the fact that this "pang" is married to "born" delights me with its Dickensian aptness.

With certain modulations, Pangborn always played the same man. Before he uttered a word, his character was in place. The quintessential tight-ass, he held himself in constant check. His posture erect to the point of distortion: back swayed, butt out, chin raised a quarter of an inch, his gestures colored by a shade of snooty effeminacy, he is the man who, if he remains on the screen long enough, will be brought down. His is a ridiculous life, a life of rules maintained at all costs, of

self-inflated dignity, of the fully buttoned suit, of obsessive cleanliness, of correctness. When he speaks, his voice swells with enunciations that are decidedly un-American. In truth, his tone bears a suspicious resemblance to that other English, sometimes known as the King's. For Americans, this accent connotes either genuine grandness or pretension. Pangborn has the voice of the small-time snob.

But why do I find Franklin Pangborn endearing? Why do I get pleasure from this altogether persnickety being who returns in one movie after another? It is partly because he is always ineffectual. In a position of real power the same character turns loathsome, but Pangborn appears time and again as the "manager" of something—store, hotel, apartment building—whose directives are subverted by the bedlam that takes place around him. And yet his desire to keep order, to maintain boundaries, to ignore the madness of others has a noble as well as pathetic dimension. Guided by decorum, the stiff man carries on, often ruffled but rarely defeated. He is the very image of threatened civility.

When I was growing up, my Norwegian mother had ideas about form, attachments to the signs of bourgeois life, which did not always match my American father's more democratic ideals. Not long ago my mother told me that, at least in Norway, one never put out candles for a dinner without having lit the wicks. The candles should not be stumps. They may be new, but the wicks must be blackened before guests arrive at the house. I asked my mother why. "I have no idea," she said, and laughed. "That's just the way it was." I now ignite my wicks before my guests arrive for a dinner party. Surely this shows a Pangbornian aspect to my personality, a will to form wholly unrelated to reason. Of course my father had no objection to blackened wicks. It is possible that he never even noticed this sign of good manners throughout his now forty-four-year marriage to my mother. Wicks fell under her domain—a domestic and feminine one.

My parents differed on the issue of fences, however, a deeper dispute that has further Pangbornian significance. My mother yearned for a fence around our property in Minnesota. For her it had nostalgic resonance, the comfort of enclosure, as well as aesthetic value. As a European, fences seemed natural to her. My father grew up as a farm boy on the prairie. He remembers barn raisings, quilting bees, and square dances. Fences reined in cows, but the idea of delineating one's property smacked of the unneighborly. Pangborn is a character defined by fences, formal divisions that articulate boundaries, difference, hierarchies. In terms of broad American mythology, these fences have a feminine quality. Franklin Pangborn's character stands in stubborn opposition to a freewheeling, democratic, masculine ideal as seen through the lens of American movies in the nineteen thirties and forties.

In an early, brief appearance in Preston Sturges's *The Palm Beach Story*, Pangborn, the manager of an apartment building on Park Avenue, leads potential tenants to the apartment of a couple played by Claudette Colbert and Joel McCrea who, having fallen on hard times, have not paid the rent. Elegant in a dark, close-fitting suit, a spotless white handkerchief protruding from his breast pocket, Pangborn serves as a foil to the near-deaf Weenie King, a western millionaire in a shabby light-colored overcoat and cowboy hat, who is accompanied by his overdressed wife. As unrefined as he is loaded, the King bangs on the walls of the corridor with his cane and shouts non sequiturs while Pangborn works hard to maintain his dignity in face of these vulgar high jinks. A Hollywood fantasy of the American West, the Weenie King doesn't give a damn about form, grammar, deportment, or fences of any kind. Pangborn answers most of the King's initial questions with the refrain "of course," interrupted by a telltale clearing of his throat, a tic that recurs in the Pangborn persona. It is as if the sum of his disapproval has lodged itself as a bit of phlegm in his throat. The Weenie King's wife notices that the apartment is dirty. The manager acknowledges this and apologizes. But the King yells that he likes dirt, that it's as natural as (among other things) "disease" and "cyclones." Sturges knows dirt is the bottom line here. Pangborn is nothing if not immaculate.

Some time after I became an adult I began to clean. I have become a zealous cleaner, a scrubber of floors, a bleacher, a general enemy of dirt and dust and stains. It is probably unnecessary to say that my mother has cleaned fervently all her life. My husband, who occasionally discovers me in these endeavors—down on my hands and knees in the recesses of some closet—has been known to cry "Stop!" He takes the long view of order and cleanliness. Why hang up your jacket if you are going to wear it in an hour when you go out? Why empty the ashtray when you can fit in one last cigar butt? Why indeed? I organize and I clean, because I love to see the lines of every object around me clearly delineated, because in my domestic life I fight blur, ambiguity, cyclones, and decay (if not disease). It is a classically feminine position, which is not to say that there aren't scores of men who find themselves in it. I don't know if Pangborn is ever seen actually cleaning in a film, but it is not necessary to see him at it. His character is spotless and obsessive, a figure of perfect order. In terms of American mythology, he is a traitor to his sex, an anti-cowboy who has joined the girls. The fun consists in rumpling him, making him sweat and stumble and get dirty.

Sturges, ever alert to the class bias of Americans who nevertheless revel in the excesses of money, makes the western Weenie King the movie's fairy godfather. The King peels off bills from a bankroll twice the size of his fist and hands them out to the lady of the apartment, whom he discovers hiding in the shower. Pangborn is left in the large living room of the upper-crusty apartment, exhausted and appalled at the rigors he is forced to endure in the course of a day's work, rigors which have left him a little crumpled.

Without western populism and its Weenie Kings, the Franklin Pangborn character could not have the same force. Uppity, pinched, urban, and sissified, he is a figure of prairie prejudices, whose elevated diction and manners are a target of ridicule. In *My Man Godfrey* we see him for only a few seconds, but those seconds are important. As Depression wish-fulfillment, this film remains among the best. Typically, Pangborn plays a fellow attempting to run things in a climate of chaos. One guesses that he is the chairman of the misguided charity committee, which has organized a scavenger hunt for the very rich. Among the "objects" the players have been asked to bring in is "a forgotten man." Carole Lombard discovers William Powell (Godfrey) in a dump by the river, and after considerable back-and-forth, the daffy but good-hearted creature played by Lombard brings the unshaven, ragged Godfrey into a glittering party of people in gowns and tails. Pangborn tests the forgotten man's authenticity by seeking permission to feel Godfrey's whiskers. (Another player has tried to cheat with an imposter.) He does this with a bow of his head, the words "May I?" and a clearing of the wonderful throat. But it is his gesture that wins my heart. He lifts his fingers, and with a flourish not seen since the eighteenth-century French court, waves a hand in the direction of the beard and declares it real. It is a beautiful moment. In that hand, we see both the rigors of politeness, which forbid intimate contact with another's body, and the distaste for a body that is unwashed, unperfumed, and generally unacceptable. After being declared the genuine article, a truly forgotten man, Godfrey dubs the company around him "a bunch of nit-wits," is hired by Lombard as a butler, and the story begins.

I have now lived in New York for twenty years and have wound up from time to time among the nit-wits. Although I have never subscribed to the bias of my hometown—that the rich are worse than other people—it is true that vast sums of money have a tendency to look ridiculous from the outside, that the spectacle of spending and playing has a tawdry appearance that turns the stomach of the born-and-bred midwesterner. For a sight of pure silliness and smug self-congratulation, little can compete with the charity ball. They knew this in Hollywood and used it. When my grandparents' farm was going to ruin in Minnesota, there were city slickers in New York who had managed to hold on to their dough. *My Man Godfrey* played for audiences in the sticks, too, audiences that feasted on the opulence of the grand New York house while they laughed at the absurdities of those who lived in it. Godfrey is the frog prince of an American fairy tale, a man whose experience of poverty transforms him. Pangborn, on the other hand, defies enchantment. The static being of bureaucratic management, he will never be transformed.

This stasis finds its best expression in W. C. Fields's *The Bank Dick*. Pangborn plays the bank examiner, J. Pinkerton Snoopington. In tight black suit, bowler hat, and lorgnette, he is the picture of a stick-in-the-mud. Pangborn's fate is to be nearly done in by Fields—Egbert Sousè. Fields's hatred of banks and bankers is well known. And although his aesthetic is anarchic, not agrarian-populist, misanthropic not humanist, his spleen against bankers must have struck a deep chord among audiences in 1940. My grandmother muttered nasty asides about banks and bankers all her life. During the Depression, she and my grandfather lost forty acres of their farm to the bank when they were no longer able to pay the mortgage. And there were many like them. It is worth remembering that torturing a bank examiner had greater fantasy value at that time than it does now.

W. C. Fields was not a great champion of women either. He plays a man whose every move is circumscribed by some foolish womanly notion. In Fieldian myth, marriage, order, codes of behavior and, above all, temperance, are invented by women to fence in the natural man's appetites. It is notable that as Sousè lures his victim, Snoopington, to the Black

Pussy Cat Café, he asks the bank examiner whether he has noticed Lompoc's beautiful girls. The examiner harrumphs that he is married and has a grown daughter "eighteen years of age." In other words, marriage has closed his eyes to other women. The man is no man. Sousè, on the other hand, continues muttering under his breath, "That's how I like 'em, seventeen, eighteen . . ." Sousè drugs Snoopington with a Mickey Finn in the Black Pussy Cat Café, half leads, half carries him to a room in The New Old Lompoc House, then either allows him to fall or pushes him out the window of that new, old establishment, hauls the bruised and disheveled examiner up the stairs once again, back into the room, and puts him to bed—all because Snoopington's sole desire in the world is to examine the books at the bank where Sousè and his future son-in-law, Og, have made an "unauthorized" loan.

Even this brief summary reveals the Dickensian spirit of Fields, a comedian whose joy in naming things is as great as his joy in the visual joke. Should we be in doubt as to the source of the filmmaker's inspiration, the bank examiner assists us. From his sickbed, the prissy Snoopington worries aloud about his wife. "My poor wife," he moans, "Little Dorrit." But, as it turns out, Sousè has underestimated the bureaucrat's willpower. The examiner somehow manages to crawl from his sickbed and arrive at the bank ready for duty. Although he is obviously woozy and a tad unstable on his feet, Snoopington's pressed suit betrays no sign of his earlier misadventures. The wily Sousè conspires to crush Snoopington's spectacles and render the examiner blind. Sousè succeeds in smashing the glasses under his foot, upon which the examiner opens his briefcase. The camera zooms in on a close-shot of its contents. The man has five extra pairs of spectacles neatly lined up within. The eyewear tells all. Driven by duty, this man comes prepared. In the finicky realm of ledgers, numbers, and accounts, he has no rival. We know, however, with absolute certainty, that he will live and die a bank examiner. Sousè, on the other hand, through mad accident and wild connivance becomes fabulously wealthy. At the end of the movie he is happily ensconced in his mansion, where his formerly abusive family now dotes on him. Fields makes a contented exit. He is off to the Black Pussy Cat Café as of old. His family declares him "a changed man."

Fenced in, stuck on a rung of the social ladder, the Pangbornian man has no appetite for change. Like most children he prefers sameness, routine, consistency. This, too, I understand. Repetition is the essence of meaning. Without it we are lost. But taken to its extreme, a love of system becomes nonsense. Franklin Pangborn played a man who worshiped the system in which he found himself, a system ruled by that Manichaean American divinity, its God and its Satan: money. Money haunts Pangborn's character in most of his movies. He does not have much of it himself, but he is victim to its charms, part of its overriding machinery, and overly impressed by its power. The quintessential manager, he's a dupe of the rich. In another Preston Sturges film, *Christmas in July,* Pangborn plays the manager of a department store, eager to please the hero and his girlfriend, who falsely think themselves newly rich and go on a shopping spree. The manager shows them a bed, a piece of furniture outfitted with an elaborate mechanism that will afford them every convenience at the touch of a button. Pangborn unfolds this wonder of American consumerism, and then in a voice at once elevated, proper, and obsequious, he says, "And then on the morrow . . ." He presses the proverbial button and the bed collapses back into itself.

I realize that it is not only the character of Pangborn that I am attached to, but the fact that he appeared in Hollywood movies during an era when dialogue still played a prominent role in the making of films, when the archaic expression "on the morrow" could be written for a laugh, when W. C. Fields could throw away a line in homage to Little Dorrit, when a Weenie King could soliloquize on his love for dirt, cyclones, and disease. It is rare now that a studio movie gives us much dialogue of any sort, and when it does, it is inevitably a language without much history, a language afraid of reference lest its audience not understand, a language deadened by the politics of the committee and the test screening. And as I bemoan this, I know full well that studios ran then and run now on an idea that is populist at heart: to get the largest number of people into the theater to see a movie that will please all or almost all—eggheads and curmudgeons excluded. But even in bad movies of the Pangborn period, talk played a larger role than it does now. I miss talk in the movies.

And the fact is that when I leave my house in Brooklyn, and I listen to people in the streets, to their locutions and their diction, to their phrases and sentences, they bear little resemblance to what I hear on-screen in "big" movies. People in my neighborhood are prey to all kinds of grandiose expressions, to malapropisms, and to flourishes of the tongue. The other day I heard a woman say to another woman, "He's nothing but a little," she paused, "a little blurb." A man sitting outside the Korean grocery in my neighborhood was musing aloud about the word *humanism*. "You call that humanism, humanistic, human beingness," he roared at anyone who would listen. Years ago, an old man sat in the Fifty-ninth Street subway and sang out a sequence of beautiful words: Coppelia, Episcopalian, echolalia . . . He had a resonant, stentorian voice that still rings in my ears. Once in La Bagel Delight, a local deli, I garbled my words and asked the man behind the counter for a cinnamon *Reagan* bagel. He looked at me and said, "We don't have any of those, but I'll give you a Pumper-Nixon." Wit and wonder live on in everyday speech. They merely go untapped in Hollywood.

The truth is that the world and our fantasies often overlap. Franklin Pangborn's character, that meticulous, preening stuffed-shirt, is not only a fiction of the screen. Once, with my own eyes, I saw his reincarnation. Several years ago, my husband and I were in Paris. He had some business there, and we were put up in a grand old hotel near the Louvre. It happened that the French actor Gerard Depardieu had taken it into his head to meet my husband, and a rendezvous was arranged in the hotel lobby. Depardieu's name had well before then become synonymous with French movies. It seemed to me that every French film I saw had that man in it. His fame was incontrovertible. The actor entered the hotel. Unlike many movie stars, he did not disappoint off the screen. He is a very large man, a formidable man, and he burns with energy. Clad in a leather jacket, his motorcycle helmet tucked under his arm, he headed toward us, his gait determined but galumphing. Depardieu exuded nothing so much as testosterone, an unvarnished, out-of-the-street maleness that, to be honest, bowled me over. From the corner of my eye, I noticed the manager of the hotel notice who had just entered his establishment. Visible but controlled excitement could be seen on his features. His face made it eminently clear that the closer Depardieu came to us, the higher our status rose in that hotel. His sharp eyes never left the celebrity. The actor arrived at our table in the lobby. He greeted my husband, the two other people with us, and me. I remember that he boomed my name with pleasure, shook my hand with the powerful grip I had expected and seated himself. The maître d'hôtel rushed over. Posture erect, chin up, scrupulously attired in his expensive dark suit and elegant tie, he tried to maintain his equanimity. He did not succeed. In his joy he began to flap his arms just a little, as if he were trying to propel himself off the ground. Then, with a dignified nod of his head in the direction of the famous one, he asked him for his drink order. Mr. Depardieu casually ordered a glass of red wine. The manager turned abruptly on his heels and speed-walked off to get it. He did not take anybody else's order. He forgot us.

As I watched him leave, I thought of Franklin Pangborn. Franklin Pangborn had been reborn in that hotel lobby, and I was there to witness his inspired silliness. The poor manager behaved in a ridiculous manner, but I felt sorry for him, too. He had breached his own rigorous standards of etiquette and had made a fool of himself. But then we all make fools of ourselves from time to time. And that, I suppose, is at the bottom of this rambling but sincerely felt tribute to the Pangbornian.

ROBERT CARLYLE

Malu Halasa

Weedy. That was my first impression of Robert Carlyle, who played the unemployed steelworker in *The Full Monty* who stripteases, with five other men, for a crowd of baying women. As he disrobed, Carlyle, thirty-five, five foot eight, performed a cocky little dance to Hot Chocolate's "You Sexy Thing," steps he had practiced under the guidance of an ex-steel mill foreman whose hobby was ballroom dancing. All the men in the film needed money but Carlyle's character, Gaz, was the most desperate. He couldn't pay his child support and his fear of losing visitation rights for his son was less New Man than outright failure.

While some British women critics noted Carlyle's sexy habit of smacking his lips, I preferred his roles. In addition to Gaz in *The Full Monty,* he was the violent thug Begbie in *Trainspotting* and the bus driver in Ken Loach's *Carla's Song*—all unlikely Hollywood matinee-idol roles. On-screen Carlyle exudes the presence of a normal bloke who could have come from a building site, which in fact he did. He had worked as painter/decorator with his dad in Scotland.

This everyday demeanor sets him apart from the current wave of British male leads. He's not Oxbridge like Hugh Grant, not smoldering street like Gary Oldman or quirky eccentric like Rowan Atkinson. The abject ordinariness of Carlyle's role in *The Full Monty* was emphasized by his clothes: baggy sweatpants and a worn nylon jacket. His low-income council flat was dominated by a scuzzy sofa, which by looks alone reeked of drink and stale fags. A visually more potent backdrop waited in Sheffield's two-up-two-down rows of Victorian terrace housing, the derelict factories picked over for scrap metal, and the junk-filled convenience store. The clothes, sofa, and city suddenly filled me with nostalgic brooding, and I was reminded of when I moved to Britain in 1980.

I had left the Lower East Side, in Manhattan, for the dour English Midlands. Margaret Thatcher had been one year in power, and I arrived in her country, dressed in a denim shirt, jeans, and white go-go boots. Most people would have headed for London, but at the airport I was met by a guitarist I knew, and soon found myself living in Birmingham, the country's second largest city, a failed automotive manufacturing center like Detroit. Most of the men there dressed like Gaz, in sweatpants or hand-me-downs. They had left school at sixteen and worked in bingo halls or curtain-rail factories or drove trucks. When they got tired of the routine, and practically no money, they reinvented themselves as pop musicians, drug dealers, even impromptu lecturers. Tommy, for example, moved from house to house, discussing Luis Buñuel and the French Surrealists. He usually stayed until everyone fell asleep in front of the electric fire, or after the last bus stopped running and it was too damn late to throw him out.

Nearly everyone was unemployed and I've never understood why the people who collected the meager government subsidy, known as "the dole"—in the early eighties roughly $45 per week—were depicted as shiftless and lazy by the Conservative government. The only economy in Thatcher's Britain was the black market and most of my friends had a scam going. It was a vital lesson for a young American about to embark on a career of freelance journalism. Gaz's flights of imagination about how to make money and his self-doubts brought back all too clearly the main lesson of underground entrepreneurialism I learned in Birmingham—don't take "no" too seriously, and find a way around barriers, no matter how high or how hidden.

As Britain transforms itself into the fifty-first American state, with an increasing obsession with U.S. foreign policy, talk shows, and Hollywood celebrities, the British working class stands out for its insularity. Because Carlyle's northern accent was so thick in *The Full Monty,* I had been told a book had been published to explain the story in Americanese. That didn't surprise me. Every time I had opened my mouth in Birmingham, complete strangers pointed out that we are two peoples divided by a common language. Every time they opened theirs, my vocabulary increased. Some words were particularly relevant to my new neighborhood of Handsworth, where turbaned men and dreadlocks bought Alphonso Indian mangoes and tinned Jamaican akee in the same shops.

One word I quickly learned was *sussed,* which meant working something out, knowledgeable. The 2-Tone gangs of

Jamaican, Irish, and Indian teenage boys, sometimes in flash, charity store suits, on the 73 bus, were "sussed." It was a compliment. The word changed its meaning entirely when used in *suss laws*, and *suss* came from *suspicion* when Bobbies stopped a dread and searched him for no good reason, an early version of zero tolerance. One thing that hasn't changed from then until now: pervasive racism.

This is the downside of white working-class Britain, a closed male culture of Us versus Them and the mythical factories, whether they were filled with working men or emptied of them, by the time I moved to Birmingham. Places, it seemed, had double meanings. I was constantly told that the historic city—where James Watt built his steam engine—had more canals than Venice. Nobody bothered to explain that the secluded waterways, between the old factories and electrical substations, were the domain of glue sniffers and skinheads. On the Lower East Side in New York there were certain corners, usually marked by a drug dealer, you knew to avoid; here territorial boundaries were invisible. As an American I slipped between them. Others weren't so lucky.

The summer after my arrival, riots broke out in Moss Side, in Manchester, and I had gone up to do a story. My first stop was the local police station, where I was shown government-issue crowd-control gear—riot shields and truncheon sticks. There had been a lot of press at the time about the cop of the future. I was then driven around an ethnic community much like the one I was living in by a racist sergeant who had nothing but contempt for the people he policed.

I returned to Handsworth and my two-up-two-down terraced house on Nineveh Road. Across the street was a little pub, the Bolton Arms, where you could run in with a pitcher and bring home Guinness or lager. It was a quiet street except for the Howler, three doors down. After he cashed his Giro— his unemployment check—and made the same trip to the pub, with his pitcher, he howled at cars and ghosts late into the night. I had always been able to sleep through this. It was no different the evening I had returned from Moss Side, when the second-hand TV and hi-fi store down my road was looted, and the off-license belonging to an Indian family had its plate-glass window punched out. The government dismissed the Handsworth riots as "copycat." I can remember the last para-graph of the story I wrote. After the high unemployment statistics I mentioned one of the jobs that was going, where a boy lost his feet in a soap-making machine. Then I finished with: "Sometimes you could wish for a war, if only for something to do." Less than eight months later the Falklands war began.

I grew up, a dozy kid, in Akron, Ohio. Not like my friend, a knowing Anglophile at the tender age of ten who scoured the Indianapolis, Indiana, TV listings for the late-night, risqué for-eign films. When the rest of his family was fast asleep he watched the Kitchen Sink Dramas. In *Saturday Night and Sunday Morning,* Albert Finney's working-class rebel has an affair with a married woman. *A Taste of Honey, The Loneliness of the Long Distance Runner, Look Back in Anger, This Sport-ing Life,* among others, were gritty, realist black-and-white films, from the late fifties and early sixties, in which women wanted to be seduced; they even enjoyed talking it, as in *Room at the Top.* By mid-decade their experience and sexual awakening dominated cinema and men took a supporting role.

Over thirty years later, London has allegedly begun to swing again, and gender politics have flipped 180 degrees. The concept of the New Man emerged in the early nineties: sensitive and caring, a diaper-changing kind of guy. He was supplanted by the current fad of Laddism popularized by the glossy men's magazines *FHM* and *Loaded,* a mix of soft porn, male toys, and adolescent humor—"the best garden shed for shagging." Many believe that New Man was a pretense and men have been selfish all along. New Lad masked a more profound shift in British economic realities. Wives, girlfriends, mothers, and sisters have become the consistently more flexible, the more desired workforce.

Both of Carlyle's most popular films, *The Full Monty* and *Trainspotting,* are about thwarted male expectation. For Gaz in Sheffield, men with babes, mobile phones, and garden sheds might as well be on the moon. *The Full Monty,* which promises full frontal nudity but doesn't deliver it, is about male incapacity. The unseen, swinging member is all hyperbole and innuendo. *Trainspotting* is thoroughly Lad. Twenty-something working-class junkie (Ewan McGregor) chooses middle-class life and commits the greatest taboo by abandoning his mates. In the new world order capitalism has won and all we have left is shopping and fucking. Those who can't tell the difference between a bag of dosh (money) and a punch in the mouth, like Carlyle's Begbie, must be thick.

Film director Antonia Bird, who cast Carlyle as the gay boyfriend in *Priest* and the socialist/anarchist turned criminal in *Face,* has complained about working-class stereotypes in the media. Other than Mike Leigh (*Career Girls, Secrets & Lies, Naked*) or Ken Loach, who gave Carlyle his first break in *Riff-Raff,* the only place filled with an abundance of working-class accents is the tawdry soaps *Brookside* and *Eastenders.* Before this genre appeared British television was strictly a middle-class affair.

There's a good chance that *Jo Jo,* the controversial four-part BBC-TV miniseries, will never be viewed by American audiences, unless HBO subtitles the indecipherable Scottish accents. *Jo Jo,* named after Carlyle's main character, charts the rise of heroin on an Edinburgh council estate in 1982, the same year the first heroin murder was committed in Maryhill, Carlyle's poor neighborhood in Glasgow.

For my friend Dave Crook, from Birmingham, the biggest change in modern Britain was the criminalization of heroin, when the drug was no longer prescribed to addicts. It is a decision that has repercussions to this day. Now all over the country there are housing estates filled with drugs and violence. Even in South Yorkshire mining villages, where a strong social fabric was once provided by the men and the pits, heroin has become a refuge for the old and young unemployed, mainly because it's cheaper than a pint of beer. In his arguments for teenage curfews and tougher punishment for drug users, the current home secretary, Jack Straw, echoes Thatcher's home secretary William Whitelaw, the architect of the "short, sharp shock" military boot camp–type prisons for young offenders. The government has finally closed the last of Whitelaw's short sharp shock facilities.

In a country with the oldest parliament and official secrets act, where there is no freedom of information or basic constitutional guarantees, TV has an enormous influence, sometimes even in the courtroom. In this capacity of Cervantes' "truth through lies," television drama documentaries tell a complex story better than the newspapers, particularly the tabloids, run by middle- and upper-class editors who think they have the common touch and feed their readers a steady diet of insidious working-class stereotypes, best typified by *The Sun*'s nudge nudge wink wink, panty-clad Page 3 Girl, ostensibly published to whet the appetite of a nation of masturbating builders.

After the 1989 Hillsborough football disaster when ninety-seven Liverpool fans were crushed to death at an FA-Cup semifinal, *The Sun* blamed football hooliganism and drunkenness, despite reckless crowd control on the part of the police. Carlyle starred as an avenging Scouse in the TV psychology thriller *Cracker,* an episode written by Jimmy McGovern, who also wrote the drama documentary *Hillsborough.* After its broadcast the Crown Prosecution reopened its investigation of the disaster. A recently discovered video from the grounds showed that the police suppressed evidence. They had been aware of the crushing but still herded an additional two thousand fans into the standing pens.

Despite Britain's reputation as a welfare "nanny" state, there have been too many incidents, too many miscarriages of justice, that suggest to anyone, no matter their race, education, or income, that self-sufficiency is far better than dependence, and sometimes you have to travel great distances to find it. Recently I was befriended by a gang of Geordie builders who regularly caught the last night bus from Sunderland in the northeast and arrived in London by dawn. They lived in the apartments they were renovating or building from scratch, using a bucket if the plumbing wasn't connected. During the recent property boom they have transformed empty West End office buildings into luxury yuppie flats. When the bloody cockney wankers became too much, the Geordies got back on the bus.

In between brick-laying and painting they told me tall tales about football, betting, and drinking. I was reminded of Carlyle and his characters. The Geordies were not apologetic or beholding. They took pride in their families and, when self-doubt didn't get in the way, their work. They built the floor of the building where now I sit and type.

Historically, my current neighborhood, near Charing Cross in London, has soaked up the blood and sweat of many migrant builders, ever since the Scots came down in the 1700s and labored for cheap to the sound of bagpipes. Unlike real life, celluloid time is deceptively linear, either costume drama or the future. In Britain, the past forever lingers. As long as there have been kings, queens, and poor governance, people dream and scheme of ways to get out from under the yoke. It is these stories Robert Carlyle tells well.

MARGARET DUMONT

Jacqueline Carey

In the foreground is the fizz of the Marx Brothers: madcap musicianship, stories that wander aimlessly from room to room, gags that sound like eruptions from some demented stream of consciousness. (From *A Night at the Opera:* "That's why I'm sitting here with you. Because you remind me of you. Your eyes, your throat, your lips! Everything about you reminds me of you. Except you. How do you account for that?") Then there is Margaret Dumont, the actress who plays the wealthy dowager.

She is planted centrally, but slightly upstage—most Marx Brothers movies still feel very stagebound. Her presence is large, white; she looks overstuffed and upholstered. Her pretty pie plate of a face seems twice as big as Groucho's, and although she is probably no more than several inches taller, the difference between the two is exaggerated by her stately posture and the way he staggers along at a sixty-degree angle. Her range of movement is minuscule: she rolls her eyes, raises her eyebrows, opens her mouth, purses her lips. Her lines, delivered in that flutey soprano, are usually brief: "Oh!" "Good gracious!" "My!" Groucho (the brother who doesn't stop talk-

ing), Chico (the brother who talks with a ridiculous Italian accent), and Harpo (the brother who doesn't talk at all) are there to shock, and she is so easily shocked. The sight of a man in his bathing suit will bring on a swoonlike cry and a throwing up of her hands. But her reaction stops there; she is too lady-like to actually collapse.

She and Groucho played their signature roles, as the genteel Mrs. Rittenhouse and Captain Spaulding, the big-game hunter, in the 1931 film *Animal Crackers*. (These were roles they briefly reprised thirty-five years later, on TV, just days before her death.) Rittenhouse was a fancy hotel in Philadelphia, and when the production was still in play form and moved from town to town, Dumont would be renamed after the local hotel at each stop. On the surface, at least, the idea is that this society lady is trying to tame a bold, barbaric, manly man by enfolding him in the suffocating embrace of her house party. Actually, she hasn't a chance, mainly because it is never clear exactly who Groucho is or what his relationship to anybody could be. "Once I shot an elephant in my pajamas. What he was doing in my pajamas, I'll never know" is not the average remark of your manly man. And his pursuit of Dumont for her money is more of an occasional pose than a motive. Neither of them plays characters in the usual sense. Dumont's roles are always too simple, and Groucho's vary too much from minute to minute.

It is pointless to analyze these movies for narrative content; you forget the plots even before they've been resolved. Rather, the films should be deciphered the way you do dreams. The opposites that Dumont and the Marx Brothers embody fall into place as easily as those in a children's picture book: wealthy/cashless, dignified/silly, old/young, female/male, Victorian/modern, moral/naughty, Protestant majority/immigrant hordes, society doctors/ingenious quackery, large staterooms/ stowing away, first-class dining/big Italian buffets, bidding conventions/outrageous cheating, high art/popular culture.

Dumont's side of the equation reflects what literary historian Ann Douglas has labeled "the feminization of culture," and certainly Dumont could have been the chairwoman of any ladies' guild, municipal improvement society, or reading club in the nation. Her taste runs to the opera, the symphony, or dark, somber representational paintings in heavy gilded frames—all terribly old-fashioned in the twenties, a turbulent sea of a decade that seemed to throw the Marx Brothers up on the beach fully formed. Ex-vaudevillians, they quickly found a larger audience, first on Broadway and then in the movie theater, at least in part because of the era's nonstop rebelliousness against the fusty and the musty. But the Marx Brothers are not overly interested in using their formidable weapons of humor and sex, jazz and swing, to rout Dumont or even to destroy the creaky old tropes she represents. In fact, what astounds me is the gentleness with which their cultural war is waged.

Marx Brothers movies became cult favorites in the late sixties. There are lots of reasons for this timing. *Duck Soup* is antiwar (well, sort of); *Horse Feathers* takes place on a college campus (well, sort of); the films only improved if you shared a joint or two beforehand; hippies were supposed to appreciate

Harpo's childlike simplicity; smart Jewish anti-heroes had become all the rage, and Groucho was the acknowledged source. But perhaps the most important reason was the way these movies framed the world as a struggle between the old (bad) and the new (good) without making it look like a zero-sum game.

To me, the sixties was the time parents decamped, literally or figuratively. Disputes could be bitter. And into this snarling psychodrama sailed the image of Margaret Dumont, mother extraordinaire.

Not that Dumont ever literally played the mother of any Marx Brother. (Their real-life birth dates: Chico, 1887, Harpo, 1888, Dumont, 1889, and Groucho, 1890.) Sometimes she is the mother of the ingenue; more often she is an aunt or just a stray rich matriarchal figure. Either she bankrolls the high jinks, as in *Duck Soup* and *Animal Crackers,* or her financial blessing is required if the right tenor (*A Night at the Opera*) or boyfriend (*The Cocoanuts*) or rest-home owner (*A Day at the Races*) is going to succeed. In any case, her wealth is key. It is shorthand in the films for the power that a parent always possesses despite the mockery or disobedience of the next generation. In the twenties a Margaret Dumont had real moral sway, if no actual economic or political power. Big Mother was still a relatively benign concept.

Certainly no one could use her power more indulgently than Dumont. Toward the end of *The Big Store* she calls out to her young nephew in that high-pitched voice infants are supposed to naturally turn to, "And, Tommy, whatever you want to do is all right with me!" What sweeter words to a young person's ears? Whenever she does oppose a plan that Youth and the Marx Brothers have endorsed, simple exposure to the true path will generally change her mind. She disinherits another nephew in *At the Circus* for his devotion to the Big Top, until it is actually set up on her lawn in Newport. As soon as the good-guy young tenor starts to sing onstage in *A Night at the Opera,* you see her in her box smiling with delight, apparently indifferent to the preceding mayhem: the pelting of the lead with hats, the orchestra breaking into "Take Me Out to the Ball Game," the scenery first flying and then ripping. Her walk and talk may be limited or inconsistent—she may turn on a dime—but that's because she is a walking, talking wish fulfillment.

Dumont is simply incapable of argument. She doesn't seem to understand half of what Groucho says. Complacently playing bridge against Chico and Harpo in *Animal Crackers,* she doesn't even notice that they are switching hands, throwing cards around, and producing an unending stream of aces or spades. Dumont can be shocked, but she can't be wounded. She is too kind, too dim, too completely rubber-skinned. This is the primary joke between her and Groucho, amplified in a million different ways. From *Duck Soup:*

GROUCHO: Not that I care, but where is your husband?
DUMONT: Why, he's dead.
GROUCHO: I bet he's just using that as an excuse.
DUMONT: I was with him 'til the very end.
GROUCHO: Hmm. No wonder he passed away.
DUMONT: I held him in my arms and kissed him.

GROUCHO: Oh, I see. Then it was murder . . . Will you marry me? Did he leave you any money? Answer the second question first.

DUMONT: He left me his entire fortune.

GROUCHO: Is that so? Can't you see what I'm trying to tell you? I love you.

DUMONT: Oh, Your Excellency.

GROUCHO: (eyebrows wiggling) You're not so bad yourself.

A worried look occasionally passes across her face, and she recoils at the word *murder*, but the next time her head dips, it is done coyly, in reaction to his transparently insincere profession of love. She is so forgiving that the condition verges on serial amnesia.

What makes all this watchable is the dignity that Dumont maintains. Take the medical examination she undergoes in *A Day at the Races*. Groucho, who is supposed to conduct the exam, is a veterinarian, not a medical doctor, as he claims, and a Dr. Steinberg is bent on exposing him. But Groucho's problem is barely suggested before it is obscured. There is a great outpouring of introductions, as Harpo and Chico also claim to be Dr. Steinbergs, and keep bowing like hinges; after much energetic hand-washing, there are several conga lines of hand-drying; then Harpo disrobes a nurse, revealing under her uniform a slip nearly identical to the uniform.

For most of this scene, Dumont is sitting upright on an examining table, at least a head taller than anyone in the room. She is wearing what looks like a dark velvet evening gown with dolman sleeves, a jeweled belt, a glittering necklace, and a monocle on a chain. Dr. Steinberg and an evil business manager are also wearing evening clothes. It is Groucho who is underdressed, in a white T-shirt and a long white apron. Harpo and Chico are wearing similar outfits, with service station logos on them. Much of the humor comes from their reluctance to touch Dumont at all, let alone in any humiliating fashion. Eventually Dumont is tipped over like an L, with her feet in the air, but her legs stay together and the hem of her dress sticks to her ankles, even when the end of the table is jacked up and down. Harpo and Chico put shaving cream on her, but it leaves no trace, as if a cream pie thrown in the face turned out to be made of cotton. When Harpo turns on the overhead sprinklers, he is the only one who gets soaked.

It is hard to imagine a more desirable parent: rich, generous, malleable but unflappable. No wonder that it now seems like less of a fantasy to talk as cleverly as Groucho than to find a mother like Dumont. But this is a one-way street. You wouldn't get much satisfaction from identifying with Dumont and inheriting overgrown children like the Marx Brothers. Today when I watch these movies with my own kids I am most aware of the odd, stubborn courage that lies behind Dumont's sweetness and good cheer. She is such a very good sport, despite the hint of mournfulness in her eyes. She is so game, so steadfast, so true. I admire her a great deal. And her dignity breaks my heart.

ANGELO ROSSITTO

Michael J. Weldon

Angelo Rossitto started acting in movies in 1927. By the end of the thirties he had worked for all the major studios: Warner Bros., MGM, Paramount, United Artists, Columbia, and 20th Century Fox. He went on to appear in "nearly 200" movies over a period of sixty years. His Hollywood career spanned seven decades, and a surprising number of his roles are still popular cult hits, but he is not even mentioned in Halliwell's *Filmgoer's Companion* or the even bigger Katz *Film Encyclopedia*. Maybe it's because he was 33 inches tall.

I found out about Angelo Rossitto as a kid reading *Famous Monsters of Filmland* magazine. Although I had seen him in some movies on TV, it was in theaters (when I was in high school) where I first saw Rossitto and knew who he was. The theater near the junior high I had attended had become the Westwood "art" theater in the mid-sixties, showing mostly foreign features (usually with sex scenes). Like so many other theaters trying to pay the bills, it became a porno theater (a shock to the suburb of Lakewood, Ohio) in the mid-seventies. In the late sixties, though, they had weekend midnight "underground" shows and I went with some friends as often as possi-

245

ble to be stimulated, confused, and often bored. At least we weren't at home watching mainstream or censored TV (or out causing trouble). Various colorful psychedelic, political, or sex-oriented shorts were mixed with starker, much harder to comprehend New York area shorts by Warhol, Jack Smith, and the Kuchar Brothers. This type of show didn't last many years and was eventually replaced by *Pink Flamingos* and other features, then *The Rocky Horror Picture Show*. Nobody needs underground films anymore, though, since every single innovation was copied by Hollywood and rock videos. These days everyone can get the same disorienting effects (and the boredom) for free and at home while watching TV commercials and learning to be perfect consumers.

The anonymous heroes who programmed these midnight shows also added really old and bizarre (often drug-related) shorts, cartoons, serials, and movies, which is how I first saw *Freaks*. I was a horror movie fanatic since I could remember and had been fascinated by the pictures of the human torso, pinheads, Siamese twins, and other real human oddities from *Freaks* in the pages of *Famous Monsters*. I already knew that *Freaks* was directed by the same man (Tod Browning) who made *Dracula* and that it had embarrassed and outraged the MGM studio execs who had backed it. It had been banned in England and was never going to show up on TV. And there was Angelo Rossitto (as Angelino)! His most famous scene is during the party when he gets up on the dinner table ("We accept you—one of us!") and offers the large communal drinking cup to the horrified Cleopatra. After so many shorts trying to shock the audience with sex, drugs, and war, nothing compared to this powerful, disturbing, and very moral Depression-era oddity.

In the early seventies, another Lakewood theater (The Homestead) tried to have a simpler midnight-movie series, screening a different feature each weekend. This is where I first saw *Night of the Living Dead* and David Friedman's *Trader Hornee*. In the late seventies, I helped (as part of the local "punk" record store) premiere *Eraserhead* as a midnight movie there (well worth the experience but a total financial washout). My second midnight Angelo screening experience was the unintentionally surreal late-forties *Scared to Death* from the tiny Screen Guild (later Lippert) studio. Bela Lugosi lurked around a house with Angelo as his assistant. Both wore identical capes and hats. *Scared to Death* (in unrealistic experimental Cinecolor!) is almost as disorienting as *Freaks* (in a totally mindless way). Both movies run just over an hour.

Over the years I've enjoyed spotting Angelo in many more places and have found out a few things about him. I only know a fraction of his credits (since he was often uncredited) and haven't seen all of those. He was born Angelo Salvatore Rossitti in 1908 in Omaha, where he sold newspapers as a kid. He went to Hollywood when he was seventeen and became a drinking buddy of John Barrymore. He appeared in a play with the then rich, popular, and respected great actor. Barrymore arranged for his friend's first film role in *The Beloved Rogue* (United Artists, 1927). Barrymore was the French beggar poet François Villon, and the German Conrad Veidt (in his Hollywood debut) was King Louis XI. Forgotten (probably lost) now, this was a major release with two of the finest actors in the world. I'd love to see it. The same year, Angelo appeared in *Old San Francisco* (Warner's, 1927), which had a musical sound track and sound effects. The tale of Spanish settlers starred Dolores Costello with Warner Oland as the (part oriental) villain.

Lon Chaney (a bigger movie star than even Barrymore) had already acted with little people several times. Midget Harry Earles (Hans in *Freaks*) was in *The Unholy Three* (1927) and John George (who considered himself simply a short man) was in *The Road to Mandalay* (1926) and *The Unknown* (1927). Angelo appeared with Chaney in two major big-budget MGM productions in 1928. *Laugh, Clown, Laugh!* was considered lost for many years (I saw a video copy in the nineties). It was based on an Italian play that had starred Barrymore on Broadway. *While the City Sleeps* was a crime movie with Chaney as a detective and Angelo as a member of Wheeler Oakman's gang. It had synchronized sound effects. Both silent films had musical scores. Chaney (who died in 1930) was only in four more features.

Another famous "lost" silent movie is *Seven Footprints to Satan* (First National, 1928) by the Danish Benjamin Christensen. I had a rare opportunity to see this fascinating feature recently (an Italian print on video). A jaded rich man is kidnapped and taken to a haunted mansion with an elevator leading to Hell (!). It features Satan, a gorilla, a wolfman, an orgy, a bit of nudity, and a bearded dwarf to help the confused hero. Angelo shows up in *Satan* quite a bit but you'll never spot him in *The Mysterious Island* (MGM, 1929), since he's one of forty little people playing fishmen underwater. Lionel Barrymore stars in the epic part-sound Jules Verne adaptation, which was codirected by Christensen. It's been shown on TNT. Another credit in 1929 was *One Stolen Night* (Warner's) about the British cavalry in the Sudan.

At the time, Rossitto was billed as "Little Angie." He also appeared in vaudeville (sometimes in blackface, which was still common at the time) and doubled for Shirley Temple. In 1932 he had what was probably his first speaking role in *Freaks* and was also in Cecil B. DeMille's epic *The Sign of the Cross* (Paramount). Easy now to find on video, *Cross* features over two hours of Christians thrown to the lions, dwarf gladiators, torture chambers, milk baths, gorillas, and some pre-code nudity. *Babes in Toyland* aka *March of the Wooden Soldiers* (MGM, 1934) is a wonderful fantasy musical comedy starring Laurel and Hardy, which used to be shown before the holidays every year on Cleveland TV. *Carnival* (Columbia, 1935) starred Lee Tracy as a puppeteer, and *Charlie Chan at the Circus* (20th Century Fox, 1936) was one of the best Warner Oland Chan movies.

After MGM disowned *Freaks* it spent many years playing the "States' Rights" circuit of inner-city theaters. They showed adults-only features (often dealing with sex and drugs) that had been denied the production code. Unlike the major-studio *Freaks*, *Child Bride* (*of the Ozarks*) (1937) was made specifically for the exploitation market. It played for years and is still shocking. The (very) underage female star takes a nude swim and her schoolteacher is tied up, stripped, and whipped for daring to challenge the local hillbilly habit of marrying little girls. Angelo (as Angelo) is a moonshine-still worker who actually saves the teacher's life.

I now realize that my earliest Angelo experiences were in classic kid movies. If I saw *Babes in Toyland* ten times as a kid, I probably saw *The Wizard of Oz* (MGM, 1939) fifteen times. It was an annual family event. One year I used my new little reel-to-reel tape recorder to tape choice parts (including, of course, the Munchkins) and played back random bits the next day during junior high classes. It cracked up some of the other kids and for some reason I escaped being sent to the assistant principal and being whipped (that came later).

In the forties Angelo started working for smaller independent studios while still appearing in roles for the majors. Horror fans are impressed by the fact that he was in two movies each with Lugosi and Karloff (all quickly made for Monogram and producer Sam Katzman). *Mr. Wong in Chinatown* (1939) and *Doomed to Die* (1940) starred Boris as an oriental detective. These movies (part of a short-lived series) weren't as good as the Charlie Chan (or Mr. Moto) movies and haven't been seen much in years. Angelo played an oriental dwarf in his first *Wong* movie. I read that Angelo ran for mayor of L.A. (!) in 1941, but I imagine it was a Monogram publicity stunt.

The pairing of Lugosi and Rossitto in *Scared to Death* had been a throwback to their days at Monogram. The visually brilliant idea of putting them both in similar capes and hats had been copied from Tod Browning's *The Unknown* (1927) with Chaney and John George. *Spooks Run Wild* (1941), written by Carl Foreman, was a Dead End Kids comedy with Nardo

(Lugosi) and Luigi (Rossitto) hanging out in a cemetery and supposedly haunting a house. In the very different *The Corpse Vanishes* (1942), Angelo is Toby, the sadistic peasant servant of mad scientist Dr. Lorenz (Bela). Lorenz sleeps in a coffin and calls Toby a gargoyle. They both use whips and kidnap young brides. In an eighties interview, Angelo said that he loved working with Lugosi and considered him a great guy but found Karloff to be cold and distant.

Despite the film work, Rossitto didn't make enough money (he was married and had two kids), so in between acting jobs he sold newspapers on Hollywood Boulevard. He said he delivered newspapers to Gen. George Patton during World War Two. At Universal he appeared briefly in the incredible hell scene in the anything-goes comedy *Hellzapoppin'* (1941) and had a major role as a (black) killer in the Sherlock Holmes movie *The Spider Woman* (1944). Gale Sondergaard keeps Angelo in a wicker trunk, letting him out to commit murders that the police consider "pajama suicides." After playing an Oriental and a black man, he was an Arab in Universal's comic full-color *Ali Baba and the Forty Thieves* (1944).

Some other forties roles were in *Lady in the Dark* (Paramount, 1944), starring Ginger Rogers, *Take It Big* (Paramount, 1944), with Ozzie and Harriet Nelson, Preston Sturges's *Mad Wednesday* (United Artists, 1947), starring Harold Lloyd, and another DeMille biblical epic, *Samson and Delilah* (Paramount, 1949). The next decade started with two 1950 period film releases from Lippert: Sam Fuller's *The Baron of Arizona*, starring Vincent Price, and the western *Bandit Queen*, starring Barbara Britton. DeMille called on Angelo once again for his all-star epic hit *The Greatest Show on Earth* (Paramount, 1952). In 1953, Angelo appeared in two very different cult movies. *Daughter of Horror* (aka *Dementia*) was a fascinating experimental, one-hour, no-dialogue, drugged nightmare movie with a murderess haunted by her abusive cop father. Once banned in New York State, it didn't open around until 1956 and was impossible to see until unofficial video copies showed up. *Mesa of Lost Women* (Howco) was a patchwork movie (partially directed by Ron Ormond) about a mad scientist with dwarf assistants creating spider women.

Jungle Moon Men (Columbia, 1955) was a Johnny Weissmuller Jungle Jim movie. There was a Cleveland TV show in the sixties that showed nothing but Jungle Jim and Bomba movies (both cheap Tarzan spinoffs). These were some of the dumbest, most childish movies ever made. Angelo was in the musical *Carousel* (20th Century Fox, 1956) and in Irwin Allen's all-star flop *The Story of Mankind* (Warner's, 1957). I didn't know for many years that Angelo was one of the big-headed aliens in *Invasion of the Saucer Men* (AIP, 1957), but I always loved when they used their needle fingers to inject teenagers with alcohol. The same year, Rossitto became one of the founding members of Little People of America. Some other members were Billy Curtis (Angelo's long-time friend) and the more famous Billy Barty. Hopefully they forced Hollywood to treat (and pay) them better.

The Blob (Paramount, 1958) features a *Daughter of Horror* clip and a marquee announcing that the movie stars Bela Lugosi. *The Wild and the Innocent* (Universal, 1959) was an Audie Murphy movie, *The Big Circus* (Allied Artists, 1959) was reminiscent of *The Greatest Show on Earth*, and *A Pocketful of Miracles* (United Artists, 1961) was Frank Capra's last movie. Angelo was in two 1962 fantasy movies. *The Magic Sword* (United Artists) was filmed in Germany and was loaded with great (for the time) special effects. George Pal's *The Wonderful World of the Brothers Grimm* (MGM) was a much bigger release. I saw and loved both of them in theaters as a kid. Albert Zugsmith's incredible *Confessions of An Opium Eater* (1962), starring Vincent Price, was screened as a midnight movie in the late sixties. Angelo played an Oriental again. *Terrified* (Crown International, 1963) was about a hooded killer. In 1967, he was in Roger Corman's *The Trip*, as one of Peter Fonda's hallucinations, and *Dr. Doolittle* (20th Century Fox). More kids became Angelo fans when he was hired by TV producers Sid and Marty Krofft. He was a regular on their ABC Saturday morning shows *H. R. Pufnstuf* (1967–71) and *Lidsville* (1971–73) and was also in the theatrical movie *Pufnstuf* (Universal, 1970). These bizarre shows were copied by McDonald's for their still-irritating Ronald McDonald/Hamburglar/Mayor McCheese campaigns.

After we ran an interview with director Al Adamson in *Psychotronic* magazine, he was murdered (then embalmed in his hot tub). Adamson had directed notorious drive-in hits starting in the late sixties and had given roles to Angelo in two of them. *Dracula vs. Frankenstein* (Independent International, 1969) was a crazed mixture of forties horror movie nostalgia, drugs, and bikers. Angelo is Grazebo, assistant to a mad doctor (J. Carroll Naish), and Lon Chaney, Jr., is a mute killer. *Brain of Blood* (Hemisphere, 1971) was an American horror movie that imitated then popular Philippines horror movies. Angelo played a brain surgeon wearing a golf cap.

Few people saw Paul Mazursky's *Alex in Wonderland* (1970), and *Mongo's Back in Town* (CBS, 1971) was a TV movie. *The Stone Killer* (Columbia, 1973) starred Charles Bronson, and the obscure *The Clones* (1973) featured John Barrymore, Jr. (then living like a lost hippy in the desert), in his last role. Another jaw dropper that I managed to see in a theater was *The Little Cigars* (AIP, 1973), a crime comedy that employed the most little people since *The Wizard of Oz*, including Billy Curtis (the costar) and Felix Silla (Cousin Itt on *The Addams Family*). In 1975, Angelo was in *The Master Gunfighter*, a western martial arts movie by Tom (*Billy Jack*) Laughlin, was on the cover of the excellent Dylan *Basement Tapes* double LP, and became a semiregular on the hit ABC series *Baretta*. From 1975 to 1978, Angelo could be seen doing what he had been doing on and off for most of his real life—selling newspapers. He also appeared on several other 1970s LPs.

In *W. C. Fields and Me* (1976), a Hollywood biography that helped end the career of star Rod Steiger, Billy Barty played Angelo to Jack Cassidy's John Barrymore, a reminder that Angelo had been in movies for nearly half a century. He provided a voice for the animated *Lord of the Rings* (1978) and was in the R-rated sex fantasy comedy *Fairytails* (1978) from Charles Band. He later said that the only role he turned down was in "a porno film." Some people still think that Herve Villechaize was in one, but he wasn't. *Studs Lonigan* (NBC, 1979) was a TV remake. He was unrecognizable as an alien in *Galaxina* (Crown International, 1980), starring Playboy Playmate Dorothy Stratton—who was murdered by her husband the day the comic sci-fi film debuted. *Something Wicked This Way Comes* (Buena Vista, 1983) was a disappointing Disney adaptation of one of Ray Bradbury's greatest books, but the famous author was on the set and autographed books for Angelo and his kids.

After loving the hyper, violent *The Road Warrior,* I wasn't too thrilled with *Mad Max Beyond Thunderdome* (Warner's, 1985), but it did feature Angelo (then in his seventies) in a last major role. He was lots of fun as the brain part of Master/Blaster, on the shoulders of Blaster (played by a six-foot-three Sydney plumber). He also appeared that year on an episode ("Fine Tuning") of Steven Spielberg's *Amazing Stories.* His last known role was as a carny barker (another nod to *Freaks*) in the voodoo segment of a very adult-themed horror anthology hosted by Vincent Price. It was called *The Offspring,* aka *From a Whisper to a Scream* (1986). Angelo Rossitto died on September 21, 1991. He was eighty-three. A devout Catholic, Angelo had two children and three grandchildren. I don't think any actor of any size had such a long and interesting career. I expect to enjoy discovering many more Angelo roles in the future and think he should be a subject of an A&E *Biography* show someday soon.

AFTERWORD

Chris Offutt

Dear Luc and Melissa,

I don't know what to tell you about the damn movie essay except that nothing's coming. I tried James Earl Jones and made a mess of him. Next I gave Harry Dean Stanton a whirl, thinking that since he was already a mess, I couldn't make matters worse. Well, I did. Then I went for M. Emmet Walsh and got absolutely nowhere. I'm embarrassed to leave you hanging at deadline time with nothing, but the fact is, I have pages of disasters.

Perhaps the problem is that I don't even go to the damn movies because the whole event runs at least forty bucks, including a babysitter. Shoot, where I grew up there was only one theater ten miles away and it showed a movie a week if we were lucky. Movies with a religious theme could run as much as a month in Kentucky. The guy who ran the theater was short, quiet, and always looked as if he'd just gotten out of a car with an exhaust leak. He did everything—sold tickets, made popcorn, ran the projector, locked up afterward, and swept the joint while the film rewound. The seats were ancient. One option was sitting in a chair with absolutely no

cushion left, having been sliced out by hoodlums years before. The alternative was a chair with the stuffing jammed into one side so that you were at a perpetual slant. My father said that he watched most movies standing in the back and leaning on the rail that ran behind the last row of chairs. My father loves the movies.

The only time I remember being alone with my father was when he took me to the movies. It happened once, when I was twelve.

I was so excited I could barely talk, and when I did, the words came out in a babbling rush that irritated Dad immensely. We drove ten miles to town, parked by the post office, walked past the barber shop and drugstore, and up a slight hill to the Trail Theatre. Its marquee angled into the street with giant black letters that said:

BILLY JACK
HLD OVER
$2 ALL SEAT

At the concession stand, he bought jawbreakers, his favorite as a child, and told me to get whatever I wanted. It took me a long time to pick, because I had never in my life seen Dad eat candy. Finally I got Junior Mints. I didn't like them, but a kid at school had an empty box and if you blew into it, you got a unique sound.

Dad went to the movies often, and had tons of instructions. Sitting in the front row was bad because you had to strain your neck to look up. Also, you had to constantly move your head from side to side to see the action. Don't sit in the back because people talk a lot. Never sit in the middle because that's where everyone wanted to sit and you'd be hemmed in. The best strategy was to sit behind a couple—not directly behind them, but beside them. That way no one could block your view, since no one would sit by the couple. The main thing was to buy movie tickets ahead of time, so that you could bypass the people standing in line.

The irony to his advice is that in 1971, in a town of five thousand, Dad and I were the only people in the theater.

Strangely, I recall only bits and pieces of the actual movie. Mainly that Billy Jack was the coolest guy I'd ever seen in my life and that I wanted to be him and hang around hippies and Indians. I wanted to wear a black hat. I wanted to live out west. I wanted to roll in the dirt and not dust off my clothes too much. I wanted to be tough and cool. Mainly I wanted to be as beloved as him.

There is a scene in which Billy Jack begins calmly removing his boots and socks. I was puzzled by this. All I could figure was that he had gotten a rock in his boot, but when he took off the other one I figured it was sand, which had a greater likelihood of getting in both boots. This mystery was cleared up when Billy Jack stood and used his feet to beat up a bad guy.

I even recall one line of dialogue. Of course, it's probably not verbatim, because I haven't seen the movie in twenty-eight years, but here it is. Billy Jack says, "I'm going to take my left foot and kick you on the right side of your jaw, and there's not a damn thing you can do about it." This is a rough paraphrase, but one thing I'm pretty sure of—he did say the word *damn*.

This was a remarkable event, since I'd never heard any curse words before except from Dad.

The image I remember most from the movie is my first view ever of a female breast. The sight just floored me. It was so fast that it didn't register what I was seeing until the camera had moved on. I couldn't believe it was allowed. I couldn't believe my father was seeing it, and even worse, that we were seeing it together. I secretly glanced at Dad to see how he was taking it and he seemed all right.

I missed the next few minutes of action as I replayed it in my head. I had never seen any part of a woman's body before. My sisters were much younger than me and didn't count. My mother was modest and maintained a strict privacy. None of my friends had gotten hold of a skin magazine yet.

After the movie was over, Dad and I went to the bathroom together, and he told me that I was an Alpha male. I nodded. He asked if I knew what that meant and I shook my head. An Alpha male is more or less the boss dog of any outfit. It meant that beautiful women liked to talk to you, and that men naturally looked to you for orders. I nodded, concentrating on hitting the urinal, which was difficult since I was standing as far back as possible due to its terrible stench. He said that there were also Beta males, who were plumbers, doctors, and engineers. And below that were Gamma males, which included everyone else. Dad assured me that I was an Alpha male. He said that there were three types, and that Billy Jack was an Alpha Two. He waited long enough for me to understand that I was supposed to ask who was an Alpha Three, which I did.

Me, he said.

Now, many years later, the old theater has long been closed and is for sale. The post office is the police station. The drugstore is closed and the barbershop burned down. There is a new theater, and admission is still only two dollars.

I recently spoke to my father by phone and mentioned my troubles about this movie essay. He suggested I write about Billy Jack, since it was the last movie he'd taken me to. I marveled at his perspective on the event. Billy Jack was our first, last, and only movie together.

Dad asked if I knew why he'd taken me to see it, and I told him no. Because it had a vicious rape scene in it, he said. He wanted me to see it so that I'd know that kind of behavior was very bad and had terrible consequences. I nodded dumbly. I didn't have the heart to tell him that I was more innocent than he thought at the time. Not only had I not seen any female anatomy at age twelve, I had no idea what rape meant.

Well, sorry to go on so long. Good luck with the book.

Sincerely,
Chris Offutt

ABOUT THE CONTRIBUTORS

JACQUELINE CAREY is the author of *Good Gossip, The Other Family,* and *Wedding Pictures.*

GINNY DOUGARY is a journalist living in London, where she interviews for *The Times Magazine.* The author of *The Executive Tart and Other Myths,* she is working on a novel.

MANNY FARBER's early film criticism appeared in *The New Republic, The Nation,* and *The New Leader,* and his essays in collaboration with Patricia Patterson were published in *Artforum, City,* and *Film Comment.* A lifelong painter, Farber has exhibited his work nationally since 1958 and has had retrospectives at the Museum of Contemporary Art in Los Angeles, Pittsburgh's Carnegie Museum, the Rose Museum at Brandeis University, and various museums in the San Diego area. He lives in Leucadia, California.

DANA GIOIA is the author of two collections of poems, *Daily Horoscope* and *The Gods of Winter,* and a collection of essays, *Can Poetry Matter?* With X. J. Kennedy, he co-edits three of the nation's most widely used literature text-books.

DAVID HAJDU, author of *Lush Life: A Biography of Billy Strayhorn,* has written for *The New Yorker, The New York Times Magazine,* and *The New York Review of Books.* His work in progress, *Children of Darkness,* deals with American folk music in the 1960s. Hajdu lives in New York and teaches at the New School for Social Research.

MALU HALASA was born in Akron, Ohio, and now lives in London. She is a journalist.

DAVE HICKEY's column, "Simple Hearts," appears regularly in *Art issues.* He is the author of *The Invisible Dragon: Four Essays on Beauty* and *Air Guitar: Essays on Art and Democracy.* He lives in Las Vegas.

SIRI HUSTVEDT lives in Brooklyn, New York. Her books include the novels *The Blindfold* and *The Enchantment of Lily Dahl,* and *Yonder,* a collection of essays.

STUART KLAWANS is film critic for *The Nation* and author of *Film Follies: The Cinema Out of Order.*

FRANK KOGAN has a dancing beat. His eye color is unknown. His height is undetermined, but you have to look up.

GREIL MARCUS is the author of *Mystery Train, Lipstick Traces,* and *Invisible Republic.* In 1998 he curated the exhibition *1948* at the Whitney Museum of American Art in New York, and contributed vocals to a version of "Double Shot (of My Baby's Love)" released on the album *Stranger Than Fiction.*

GEOFFREY O'BRIEN's books include *Hardboiled America, Dream Time, The Phantom Empire, Floating City,* and *The Times Square Story.*

CHRIS OFFUTT is the author of two books of short stories, *Out of the Woods* and *Kentucky Straight;* a memoir titled *The Same River Twice;* and a novel, *The Good Brother.* His work has received numerous honors, including a Guggenheim Fellowship and a Whiting Writer's Award. After many years of travel, he has recently returned to his home county in eastern Kentucky, where he teaches writing at Morehead State University.

RON PADGETT's recent books include *New & Selected Poems, Creative Reading: What It Is, How to Do It, and Why,* and a translation of *The Complete Poems of Blaise Cendrars.* The recipient of fellowships from the Guggenheim Foundation and the National Endowment for the Arts, Padgett serves as publications director of Teachers & Writers Collaborative and teaches imaginative writing at Columbia University.

MELISSA HOLBROOK PIERSON once believed watching movies was how you stayed alive. She is the author of *The Perfect Vehicle.*

ROBERT POLITO is the author of *A Reader's Guide to James Merrill's* The Changing Light at Sandover; *Doubles,* a book of poems; and *Savage Art: A Biography of Jim Thompson,* for which he received the National Book Critics Circle Award in biography. He edited the Library of America volumes *Crime Novels: American Noir of the 1930s and 1940s* and *Crime Novels: American Noir of the 1950s.* He is director of the graduate writing program at the New School for Social Research in New York City.

MARK RUDMAN's books include *The Millennium Hotel, Realm of Unknowing: Meditations on Art and Suicide and Other Transformations,* and *Rider,* which received the National Book Critics Circle Award. He has translated Boris Pasternak's *My Sister Life,* Euripides' *Daughters of Troy,* and is currently working on palimpsests of Horace and Ovid. His most recent book, *Provoked in Venice,* completes a poetic trilogy.

LUC SANTE is the author of *Low Life, Evidence,* and *The Factory of Facts.* He was a movie critic for a few years a long time ago.

CHARLES SIMIC is a poet, essayist, and translator. He teaches American literature and creative writing at the University of New Hampshire. His latest book of poems is *Walking the Black Cat,* and he has a new book of essays and memoirs called *Orphan Factory.* He won the Pulitzer Prize for poetry in 1990.

PATTI SMITH is a singer, songwriter, and poet who lives in Michigan. Albums from the Patti Smith Group include *Horses*, *Easter*, and *Wave*; *Dream of Life* was recorded with her late husband, Fred Sonic Smith. She is the author of *Early Work: 1970–1979* and *The Coral Sea*.

PATRICIA STORACE is the author of *Heredity*, a book of poems, and *Dinner With Persephone*, a travel memoir about Greece. Her work appears frequently in *The New York Review of Books* and *Condé Nast Traveler*.

CHRIS TSAKIS, who grew up blue-collar in Lindenhurst, Long Island, was a punk before you were a punk, playing guitar in two seminal New York outfits, The Nihilistics and, later, Missing Foundation. He moved to New Jersey in 1984 and shortly thereafter began co-hosting "The Nightmare Lounge" with cartoonist Kaz on free-form WFMU. Five years later he gave birth to "Aerial View," a phone-in talk show now in its tenth year—on the same station. He currently lives in Hoboken, occasionally channeling the spirit of Timothy Carey.

JOHN UPDIKE is the author of numerous novels, short story collections, volumes of poetry, and a play. He has contributed to many periodicals, most notably *The New Yorker*, which has been publishing his stories, poems, and book reviews for over four decades. He has won the National Book Award and the Pulitzer Prize for fiction.

MICHAEL J. WELDON (from Cleveland, where he used to enjoy midget wrestling) is publisher and editor of *Psychotronic Video* magazine, which features interviews with actors, directors, and musicians, and columns and reviews. He has been writing reviews of cult, horror, and exploitation movies since the late seventies when he worked in a "punk rock" record store, and he now lives next to some cows in Sullivan County, New York, with his wife, Mi Hwa. *The Psychotronic Encyclopedia of Film* and *The Psychotronic Video Guide* are collections of his reviews, and he is working on a book about music of the twentieth century. He has presented programs of rare movies in a half dozen countries, and his favorite song is still "Papa Oom Mow Mow."

JONATHAN WILLIAMS is a poet, essayist, sometime photographer, and publisher of the Jargon Society since 1951.

LINDA YABLONSKY is an art critic based in New York and the author of *The Story of Junk*, a novel. She is also the creator and host of NightLight Readings, a monthly writers-in-performance series at The Drawing Center. When she isn't talking about movies or looking at art, she's writing a new work of fiction.

PERMISSIONS ACKNOWLEDGMENTS

INDEX

(*Italicized* page number refer to illustrations)

Index

Index